How to Love a Libra

a Libra

Real life guidance on how to
get along and be friends with
the seventh sign of the Zodiac

How to Love a Libra

Real life guidance on how to
get along and be friends with
the seventh sign of the Zodiac

Mary English

Winchester, UK
Washington, USA

First published by Dodona Books, 2012
Dodona Books is an imprint of John Hunt Publishing Ltd., Laurel House, Station Approach,
Alresford, Hants, SO24 9JH, UK
office1@jhpbooks.net
www.johnhuntpublishing.com
www.dodona-books.com

For distributor details and how to order please visit the 'Ordering' section on our website.

ISBN: 978 1 78099 613 4

A CIP catalogue record for this book is available from the British Library.

Design: Stuart Davies

Printed and bound by CPI Group (UK) Ltd, Croydon, CR0 4YY

We operate a distinctive and ethical publishing philosophy in all
areas of our business, from our global network of authors to
production and worldwide distribution.

CONTENTS

This book is dedicated to my son S. G.
Thank you for being lovely

Acknowledgements

I would like to thank the following people:

My son for being the Libran that makes me always look on the other side and to whom this book is dedicated.

My Taurus husband Jonathan for being the most wonderful man in my world.

Mabel, Jessica and Usha for their Homeopathic help and understanding.

Laura and Mandy for their friendship.

Chico Holton for being my musical Libran friend.

Donna Cunningham for her help and advice.

Judy Hall for her inspiration.

Alois Treindl for being the Pisces that founded the wonderful Astro.com website.

Judy Ramsell Howard at the Bach Centre for her encouragement.

John my publisher for being the person that fought tooth and nail to get this book published and all the staff at O-Books including Stuart, Nick, Trevor, Kate, Catherine, Maria, Elizabeth and Mary.

Mary Shukle, Liz Warren, Oksana and Mark Edwards for their welcome editing eyes…

And last but not least my lovely clients for their valued contributions.

Introduction

This series of books was born from me wanting people to understand my sign of the Zodiac, which is Pisces, and gradually grew into a portrait of each sign of the Zodiac.

When I had finished *How to Survive a Pisces*, my clients and friends asked me, 'When are you going to do *my* sign?' and it was then I realised I'd got a lot of work to do!

I work in private practice, helping clients with divorce, break-ups, lack of work, personal issues, sadness, grief, curiosity or just plain discontentment, and I do my best to help them back on a path to recovering their soul's mission. I love my work!

As I'm also a qualified Homeopath, I help clients get back to a state of wellness.

I write an Astrology column for Talk Radio Europe, and every two weeks give live, on air, the bi-weekly 'stars'.

Everyone likes to know what's going to happen with their star sign...and everyone knows what sign they are, unless they're born close to when the signs change; then they could be one sign or another. This is when an experienced astrologer or good astrological programme will let you know the truth because you can't be two signs, and there is no such thing as a cusp. You're either one sign...or another.

As I had started at the last sign, I decided to go backwards...so here we are at Libra, the sign of the scales.

I'm reasonably qualified to write about this sign, as I have one at home. I gave birth to one child, a Libra. He's not remotely interested in Astrology but then children aren't that interested in things their parents get up to, especially if they seem out of date.

However, regardless of whether he follows Astrology or not, I know that understanding his Sun sign makes and made a huge difference to me feeling confident about parenting him.

I thank my lucky stars that I read Linda Goodman's *Sun Signs* before and after he was born, and permanently imprinted in my brain are the words: 'Never give him a choice. He hates to make a decision. If there's anything a Libran child hates more than making up his mind, it's having to make up his mind in a hurry.'[1]

So when he was little, instead of confusing him with lots of alternatives, we did things together and did one-thing-at-a-time, and we have never had an argument about clothes or homework.

Definition of Astrology

Astrology is the study of the planets but not in the astronomical sense. Astrologers look at the planets and record where they are from the viewpoint of the Earth and divide the sky into 12 equal portions. Those portions start at the spring equinox of 0° Aries. We use astronomical information but the difference between astronomy and Astrology is that astrologers use this astronomical information for a different purpose.

We use it to add meaning to our lives.

Originally astronomers and astrologers were the same species but as science progressed, astronomers broke away and focused only on the planets themselves, not on their meaning.

Astrologers believe that we are all connected.

'As above, so below.'

Just as we are all united as beings from the same human race, astrologers believe we are all connected in some way to everything around us...and the planets above us aren't just random happenings; they are there to guide us.

To understand a star sign or more accurately a Sun sign, we have to know a little bit about the history of Astrology and how we've got to where we are today.

People have always been interested in their surroundings, and early nations were fascinated with the night sky. Have you ever looked up at the night sky and wondered what all those dots of light were? Well, they did too and that's where Astrology started.

A Brief History of Astrology

Christopher McIntosh, a historian, tells us in his *The Astrologers and Their Creed* that Astrology was discovered in what is now called the Middle East: Iraq.

It was the priests of the kingdom of Babylonia who made the discovery, which set the pattern for the development of astronomy and of the zodiacal system of astrology that we know today. For many generations they had been meticulously observing and recording the movements of the heavenly bodies. Finally they had, by careful calculation, discovered that there were besides the Sun and the Moon, five other visible planets which moved in established courses through the sky. These were the planets that we now call Mercury, Venus, Mars, Jupiter and Saturn.

In the beginning the stars and planets were regarded as being actual gods. Later, as religion became more sophisticated, the two ideas were separated and the belief developed that the god 'ruled' the corresponding planet.

Gradually, a highly complex system was built up in which each planet had a particular set of properties ascribed to it. This system was developed partly through the reports of the priests and partly through the natural characteristics of the planets. Mars was seen to be red in colour and was therefore identified with the god Nergal, the fiery god of war and destruction.

Venus, identified by the Sumerians as their goddess Inanna, was the most prominent in the morning, giving birth as it were, to the day. She therefore became the planet associated with the female qualities of love, gentleness and reproduction.[2]

These early priests built tall towers and looked at the night sky to make their records. It was handy that the skies over Babylon

3

were clear of light pollution, buildings, or even tall hills or mountains, so they got a clear view.

Astrology Today

Fast-forward a few thousand years to today and Astrology is used for a number of different reasons:

1. As a form of divination: hopefully to aid preparations for hard times ahead;
2. As a form of religion: something to worship;
3. For light relief: something to take one's mind off current affairs.

Or the category that I work within:

4. To add some meaning to people's lives and help them feel more secure in themselves and in control of their emotions. You could say it is a form of spiritual counselling.

There is still a lot of confusion about the words we use in Astrology. 'Horoscope' being one of them.

In my dictionary 'horoscope' is a noun and means: 'Forecast of person's future from diagram showing relative position of stars at birth.'

Rae Orion in her *Astrology for Dummies* defines 'horoscope' as: 'A complete astrological chart, calculated for a specific time and place and including the Sun, the Moon, and the planets – a birth chart. The word is also used to refer to the daily or weekly predictions that appear in newspapers and magazines.'[3]

What I will be talking about here in this little book is horoscopes or birth charts and not predictions.

There are two types of Astrology practised in the West: Tropical Astrology, which gives the position of a planet by sign; and Sidereal, which gives the position by constellation. Over

4,000 years ago, on the vernal equinox, the first day of spring, the Sun was in the constellation of Aries. Now because of the Earth wobbling on its axis and a thing called 'precession', the Sun enters in the sign of Aries but in the constellation of Pisces.

I practise Tropical Astrology, taking into account that as far as the planets are today, they've shifted. Both systems have value; there is no 'right' or 'wrong'. I just prefer Tropical.

So let's find out a little bit about Libra, and how to love one.

Mary L. English

Bath 2012

Chapter One

The Sign

An online YouGov survey of 2,090 people in 2010 found that 2% don't know what star sign they are.[4] Which, when you think about it, means 98% of people do know. If that's the case, how did they find out their sign? They weren't born knowing. Most people read about their signs in newspapers and magazines and they all print different dates.

The correct dates are when the Sun moves into the part of the sky that we call Libra. This generally occurs between the dates of 23rd September and 23rd October. I say 'generally' because it all depends where you were born, and at what time of day as everything moves every few hours. There is no such thing as a cusp; you are either one sign or another. You can't be both.

If you were born at 12.02am on 23rd September 1989 in Canberra, Australia, you'd be a Virgo, but if you were born at the same time in Baker's Lake in the Northwest Territories (above Canada) you'd be a Libra.

The same applies to 23rd October: if you were born in the same location in Baker's Lake at 4.02am you'd be a Scorpio. So make sure you get your chart made up accurately if you were born on the day that the signs were changing.

Libra is represented by the scales, and its glyph or symbol is a horizontal line with an arched line above it (see Chapter Two, How to Make a Chart). It is the only sign of the Zodiac that isn't a living thing. The only inanimate object. But those scales are important for this Sun sign as they represent the challenge between personal desires and the needs of others. Between the world of ideas, and the world of reality. Between that which is living and that which is without life. A delicate balancing act.

Each sign of the Zodiac has a planet that looks after it. We call it their 'ruler'. The planet that rules Libra is Venus, and the Babylonians originally named it after their Goddess Inanna.

Goddess Inanna

This Goddess was allocated to the planet that the Babylonians saw rising and falling in the sky. Diane Wolkstein (a Scorpio) talks about her origins in *Inanna, Queen of Heaven and Earth: Her Stories and Hymns from Sumer*:

> Inanna's name means 'Queen of Heaven' and she was called both the First Daughter of the Moon and the Morning and Evening Star (the planet Venus). In addition, in Sumerian mythology, she was known as the Queen of Heaven and Earth and was responsible for the growth of plants and animals and fertility in humankind. Then, because of her journey to the underworld, she took on the powers and mysteries of death and rebirth.[5]

Nick Campion (a fellow Pisces) tells us more about Venus in his *The Dawn of Astrology*:

> It oscillates between being a bright morning star, rising before the sun, and an equally striking evening star, appearing after dusk...Whether as morning or evening star, at its maximum distance from the sun, there are moments when Venus will briefly be the only visible star in the sky, dominating the heavens as a brilliant point of light. It is these periods that are separated by 584 days and five 584-day Venus cycles are completed in 8 years to the day, an observation which was recognised from the third millennium onwards in the use of an eight pointed star as Inanna's emblem.[6]

As Astrology progressed across the globe, it went via Rome and it was there that the name of the planet changed to Venus, and she's been called Venus ever since.

The Astronomy of Venus the Hot Planet

Venus is bright enough to be seen from the Earth with the naked eye. Like the Moon, it goes through phase changes, appearing as a bright light illuminated by the Sun, to a larger crescent, as it gets nearer to us, with some of it in shadow.

'Its surface is over twice as hot as your kitchen oven at 462 °C day and night. It is the closest planet to the Earth and similar in size.'[7]

Astronomers don't call the Moon a planet; they call it a satellite or celestial body. But Astrologers call *all* the bits we use planets, and sometimes astrologers call the Sun (which is technically a star) and the Moon 'lights' or 'luminaries': natural light-giving bodies.

Like the Earth, Venus is also made of rock but its climate has 'gone out of control'.[8]

It is surrounded by a dense layer of clouds and underneath these clouds the Russian probe 'Venera 7' landed on the surface in 1970 and discovered the extreme heat temperatures on the planet's surface. Other missions and probes sent back information but it wasn't until 1990 that a US spacecraft called 'Magellan' orbited with cloud-penetrating radars and found out that the surface is totally dry with evidence of volcanic eruptions.

Every now and then Venus' orbit means it crosses over the Sun. Sort of like a mini-eclipse. It can't block out the Sun like the Moon can, as it's further away from us and only makes a black mark as you're looking at the Sun, which I don't recommend as that's dangerous to your eyes; you need to use special lenses.

This last happened in June 2004. The next visit will be in June 2012 – and I'll be watching but this book will be published after that event – then again in 2117, which is a bit of a long wait!

Venus the Goddess of Love

'Whether life is worth living depends on whether there is love in life.' R. D. Laing

When Astrology progressed across to Greece, the original Greek names for Venus were based purely on its appearance in the sky: 'Herald of the Dawn' or 'Herald of Light' and sometimes 'Star of the Evening', because people saw it as visible early in the day and then as it orbits it becomes visible again early in the evening. They called their Love Goddess Aphrodite.

Then when Astrology made it to Rome, they called her Venus the Goddess of Love. She was the lover of Adonis, best mates with Eros the winged god, and just to complicate things, got caught in bed with Mars, even though she was married to the God Vulcan. Some things never change!

Astrologers associate Venus with love, flirtation, seduction, art, beauty, luxury, harmony and pleasure, but don't just take my word for it. What do other astrologers say about Venus?

Here's Christopher McIntosh again, in 1971:

Originally associated with the goddess of the Babylonians, Venus has always been associated with motherhood and hence with love and the sexual act. Traditionally it is benefic.

According to Ptolemy c AD 90 – c AD 168, 'When Venus rules alone in a position of glory, she renders the mind benignant, good, voluptuous, copious in wit, pure, gay, fond of dancing, abhorring wickedness.'

She's obviously a fun sort of gal!

Here is Libran Tracy Marks in her *Planetary Aspects: From Conflict to Cooperation* in 1987: 'Your focal Venus will contribute to your ability to remain aware of other people's needs, to express yourself tactfully, to cooperate easily, and to maintain smooth and comfortable interactions.'[9]

There is no doubt that astrologers agree with the qualities of Venus. Here is Howard Sasportas in his *The Inner Planets* talking about Venus to a group of Astrology students in 1993:

For many years I talked about Venus mainly in terms of the Eros principle, the urge for union and relationship which exists in all of us...I first want to examine Venus as a significator of our value system, of what we find beautiful and desirable. Venus is an indicator of what we value or desire, of those things which we feel will give us pleasure or make us more complete and more whole.[10]

There's no change to her attributes, just the language changes a little.

Here's Libran Caroline Casey in her *Making the Gods Work for You* in 1998:

When Venus walks into the room, everyone becomes wittier...She reminds us to honor our individual affinities – those people, colors, tastes, animals, art forms, and interests to which we are drawn...Venus is the invisible force of attraction, love, kinship, art, and relationship.[11]

Donna Taylor, another Libran lady talking about Venus, says in her *How to Use the Healing Power of Your Planets*:

Since Venus is famous for being the planet of love and beauty and all things lovely we may think her influence upon our health and well-being is automatically benevolent. But appearances can be deceptive, never more so than where the beautiful outward appearance of Venus is concerned...if her needs are ignored her effect upon health can be quite brutal. This is largely because she governs love and pleasure, and if we don't receive enough love we quickly wither and die.[12]

Because of these associations, and the rulership system, Libra takes on some of these qualities, which we will now discuss in more detail.

Beauty

One of the qualities ascribed to Venus is beauty, so I asked a few Librans for their views on beauty. What did they *feel* the word 'beauty' meant for them?

Heather is 45 years old and works as an Aura-Soma colour therapist in private practice in the UK. She uses colour to help her clients feel empowered. I asked her for her definition of beauty:

'Beauty is the way a person is, their smile, the warmth of their eyes. The way they are. It is also something that can take your breath away. Most often mother nature supplies the most beauty.'

Angela is a mum and full-time trainer for a large business corporation. She is in her mid thirties and lives in a rural area and commutes to work every day in the city. I asked her what she thought about the word 'beauty':

'Emotionally moving, peaceful, yet exciting.'

Michael is in his late twenties and works part-time as a retail assistant while pursuing his 'dream job'. He also helps run a city farm that is organically and environmentally conscious. I asked him for his views on beauty:

'Beauty is elegance, grace, the realization of potential, that which transcends words, something which is ineffable. Beauty is a concept that is personal in the minds and hearts of everyone, yet touches us all in the same way. Beauty is inspiring, uplifting, a raison d'être. Beauty is all around us and yet not noticed by all. Beauty is the face

of God. Beauty is the pinnacle of life. Beauty is truly in the eye of the beholder...and as such lies in everything.'

Gwen is in her late thirties and is mother to two sons. She's also a part-time art therapist in a Steiner school:

'Beauty is elegance, simplicity, honesty, integrity, strength, harmony and grace.'

Lola is a territory manager for a large international company in the USA:

'Beauty can be anything: a scene in the country, a picture, an object, an article of clothing, the inner beauty of a person's soul, a pretty girl or a handsome man, just something/someone that strikes one with awe.'

As you can see, none of these Librans has a problem describing the word 'beauty'.

Fairness

As the symbol for Libra is the scales, and is the only sign of the Zodiac that isn't something living, having balance and being fair are important. Again I asked some Librans for their views, because after all, they are the ones that know themselves best.

My question was: 'How important is being fair for you?'

Here is Celia, a housewife in her late forties, a Homeopath and proof-reader. She lives deep in the country in the UK, miles from 'civilisation' on a farm with her farmer husband, teen sons and daughter.

'Being fair to me means putting oneself on an equal plane to all others.

I like to be seen to be fair and try hard to be but there is a part of my brain that is very business-like in a competitive way in that I do like achieving and sometimes the "all's fair in love and war" mentality prevails – more so when I was younger and in a competitive environment where the bright stars got on and the rest stayed where they were. Only really learnt to be truly caring and sharing through homoeopathy which came long after a successful business career; even with young children I was working the stock market as a day trader and that is a pretty cut throat and uncaring place to be – but exhilarating too!'

Here is Lionel, a retired historian who lives in London:

'Very important. Trying to ensure a measure of acceptance all round.'

Here is Sammy, a mum and home birth Duala:

'Being fair is the bane of my life! It drives me, and defines my existence. It has caused me to lose friends and alienate myself from people I once cared about. If I see an injustice, I feel compelled to speak up. I might stuff that impulse down for a while, but it always bubbles back up, usually accompanied with a big dose of righteous anger. I am nothing if not fair. I always look at every side of a situation, and if I am having a conflict with someone, I end up spending a lot of time reflecting on my own failings or "buttons" to see if I am the one at fault. My partner tells me that I should stop this self-critiquing, and I know in my heart that my feelings are just that, and don't need to be rationalised, but that doesn't stop my brain from trying.'

Arguments vs Discussion

There is one thing that can easily set a Libra off into an eternal spin, and that is when other people argue, and they have to be the witness to this arguing. I asked a number of Libra people how they felt when people argue and here are their replies:

> *'It physically and mentally stresses me.'*
> *'I get upset; my heart races.'*
> *'Anxious.'*
> *'Don't like to see or hear people arguing, will distance myself.'*
> *'Uncomfortable – I want to stop it and make it better for them.'*

Celia tells us in more detail how she feels when people argue:

> *'Awful – sets my heart pounding and my brain racing as to how I can sort it out for them. If it becomes violent with a lot of swearing I just want to get as far away as possible. I feel very uncomfortable even in a bad atmosphere and cannot concentrate in case it "kicks off" and I need to flee – torn between the need to help and the need to disappear.'*

So two things are happening for her: one, the need to help, and the other to flee. What a conundrum! An Aries wouldn't even think; they'd be in there, sorting things out…and the other Fire signs would also be wading in, shouting louder, trying to control the situation.

The Water signs would already have left the room to 'get help'…and the Earth signs would be watching in disbelief, taking it all in, remembering who did what and who said what and when it's over would then step in and clear up the mess…while the other Air signs would do a bit of yelling, then tackle one person in the group who they know well, and get *them* to break things up.

Michael has similar thoughts and feelings about arguments:

> *'I absolutely hate it. I think it's extremely sad and it makes me feel the world isn't such a nice place to be in. Internally I sort of cower away from it. If I can get away from it I will. Otherwise I try and*

block it out somehow. It impacts on my peace.'

Like everything in life, there is a paradox. As much as Libra hates arguing, they also can be highly argumentative and will correct you mercilessly if they think you're 'wrong' about something.

A Libra will love what they call a 'discussion' and it can get quite heated sometimes, if they think they haven't been understood, or you've ignored a point they've raised. They also have a quick repartee in back-chat and can be really swift to point out something, or remind you of something you might have said years ago that relates to the present 'discussion' so you're floundering and on the defensive. This is an Air sign trait that only Air signs can manage. And if you agree with what they've said, they will point out that only a moment ago you were saying something completely different, so how come you're now agreeing? It's at this point that I switch off, but an Air sign (Gemini, Aquarius and Libra) will just have got going and want to continue the 'discussion' as they enjoy the batting around of ideas, and the excitement of the verbal chase.

Angela expanded on this a bit for me:

'Strangely, most people think I'm really decisive, simply because I argue a point passionately but, as you know, like many a Libran, I can be open to persuasion – unless the decision is about fairness!'

Ah, decisiveness, the eternal bane of a Libran's life...

Indecision

This is one of Libra's most acute worries – that they won't be able to 'make up their mind'. It's not something physical, like 'Will I be able to lift that box?' It's more 'What will happen if I *don't* lift that box? Are there any other ways of me moving it?' The mental torture can go on for hours, days, weeks.

This is mostly when a Libra client is likely to make an

appointment. When they 'have' to make a decision about something, be it marriage, new job, house move, having or not having children.

I've had Libra clients tie themselves in knots with the pondering, and the only solution is to make one decision at a time.

Some of the real quotes from my clients came from a teeny questionnaire I sent them and I had to laugh when I asked one (very nice) Libra lady for her views and days later she emailed back:

'Hi Mary, I'm really sorry for not yet completing your Libra questionnaire! I keep procrastinating...which is rather ironic. And then I forget. I'll do it on Fri night.'

I had written on the questionnaire that she shouldn't think *too* much about her answers, because I know that too much thinking gets Librans into a real state, and I just wanted gut or first reactions.

Michael gave me an in-depth view of how indecisive he is:

'Absolutely awful! OK, so my problem is that I can always see the pros and cons to everything. This might mean, in an argument, I never feel that I truly "win" it as such, as I can always see the other person's point of view.

The problem with this is, I don't ever see one single truth. I believe truth is on many different levels and as such many points can be relevant and appropriate; however, I do believe that there are higher truths than others. Too often, if I am in a debate/argument, I can concede the other person's points as "a truth"; however, this often masks my point, as a truth of the bigger picture. In short, there are no blacks and whites...only greys...and yet everyone I interact with only sees things in blacks and whites, so whilst I always see everyone else's point – even if it is of lesser validity than mine – they rarely see mine as they are so stuck in theirs!'

He then tells me what happens when he goes shopping.

'When at a supermarket, or trying to purchase something, I always look for the best value. So I am constantly comparing the price per gram or per unit of something, to try and save a few pence, but even then, there are other factors to consider such as the quality, whether it is worth paying more. My problem in buying clothes and items of luxury is that I can see the good points in every decision. This somewhat hinders me from being clinical as I am literally stopped from being able to make any decision.'

And it's not just shopping that causes difficulties:

'I am forever asking for approval or confirmation in my life. Whether it be making a phone call in a busy supermarket store to ask which is best of products a, b or c...when there is not that much in-between them; or making life decisions, such as which job to go for, or which such-and-such to approach. It literally cripples me, and however much I try to shake myself out of it, I can literally spend minutes in front of the same objects in shops, my head spinning as to which one to choose.'

I have been a witness to this kind of state (see 'Your Libra Child' in Chapter Eight) and it's not a pretty sight.

Janice is a conference co-coordinator and mother to two kiddies. She tells us about her ability to decide:

'Not so good. I weigh up the results of each choice and where I would end up in either case. I also take account of how I feel about it, what's the vibe? E.g. renting a flat: location – is it convenient, safe? Upside or downside of a smaller place etc, but would I be happy to live in it, does it have the right vibe? If something doesn't

feel "right", however sensible, I would hesitate to make a decision and would stall.'

Angela also has dreadful problems with indecision:

'I used to be indecisive, but now I'm not so sure! Ha! Ha! Generally I'm paralysed by too many options; it doesn't matter how big or how small the decision is. I joke that I won't even buy something from a shop that doesn't do returns. I'm genuinely often not sure what I want or prefer. I can't even analyse what happens in my head as I don't think my brain is involved – and when it is, it doesn't seem to bring much clarity! Like most people, the more stressed I am, the less I can decide anything. It doesn't really matter what size the decision is.'

Even though Lola can make rapid, executive decisions at work, for domestic purposes she gets flummoxed:

'Making up my mind can be difficult. It depends on the mood. Sometimes I can go out and see exactly what I want and make the purchase. Other times I can't decide, e.g. looking for a new sofa for my lounge. Six months I have been in my new home and I still cannot make my final decision.'

Their indecision is not based on an inability to think things through; it's because they want to be fair, and to truly be fair you need to look at more than one option...and this can be the Libran failing. Maybe tossing a coin would be more productive?

Chapter Two

How to Make a Chart

Before the invention of computers, making a birth chart was a complicated, mathematical nightmare (in my opinion).You had to find the longitude and latitude of the place of birth, convert local time to GMT, calculate positions of the Ascendant, and planets in houses and various degrees of this and that.

Learning Astrology never became a reality for me until computer programmes came onto the market...and off I went. My auntie used to make charts by hand, and she was good at maths. I'm too impatient to spend time calculating things.

Luckily all of that hard graft has now changed. There are numerous good astrological programmes, but we will be learning from a free resource based in Switzerland, so we can rely on its accuracy.

Please note, there are plenty of Internet websites that give free information, but their accuracy can't be guaranteed so I will be using the only one that I've found that is consistently tip-top.

Go to www.astro.com and make an account.

Then click on the link at the top of the page that says Free Horoscopes.

Next scroll down the page until you can see the section on the right called Extended Chart Selection. Click on this.

You are now on a page that says:

Birth data
Options
Image size
Additional objects

Under Birth data your name should appear; if it doesn't, click on 'Add new person' and pop your birth data in. You will need the date, time and location of birth.

We're going to make the birth chart of a wonderful astrologer called Marc Edmund Jones who developed a way of interpreting birth charts based on their shape. Something that I'm very interested in.

He was born on 1st October 1888, in St Louis MO, USA at 8.37am.

If you input his data, you can follow along with what I've written here and see if we end up with the same chart.

On this Extended Chart Selection page, there is only one piece of information that I want you to change.

Where it says **Options**, underneath it says 'House System'.

We want to use the Equal House system because the default is set to Placidus, which is too confusing for a newbie and won't work for the suggestions I've given in Chapter Five on the houses.

So scroll down the house systems to the 6th choice, which says 'equal house' and click on that.

You're now ready to click on the blue button on the right-hand side that says 'Click here to show the chart'.

Click on that and your chart should look like this:

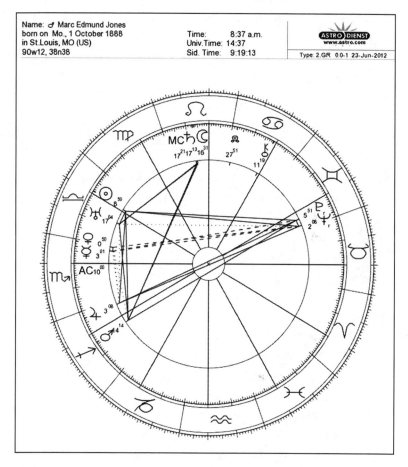

In this example, Marc has a Scorpio Ascendant (don't come too close, I'm mysterious!), Sun in the 11th (be my friend, join my group) and Moon in Leo (don't ignore me, lavish me). When you make your chart, there will be a number of lines in the centre going from planet to planet. They represent either easy or challenging mathematical associations between each planet and are called Aspects. Ignore them.

We only want three pieces of information. The **sign** of the **Ascendant**, the **sign** the **Moon** is in and the **house** the **Sun** is in.

This is the symbol that represents the Sun:

And this is the symbol for the Moon:

The houses are numbered 1–12 in an anti-clockwise order.

These are the shapes representing the signs, so find the one that matches yours. They are called glyphs.

Aries ♈
Taurus ♉
Gemini ♊
Cancer ♋
Leo ♌
Virgo ♍
Libra ♎
Scorpio ♏
Sagittarius ♐
Capricorn ♑
Aquarius ♒
Pisces ♓

The Elements

To understand your Libra fully, you must take into account which element their Ascendant and Moon are in. Each sign of the Zodiac has been given an element that it operates under: Earth, Air, Fire and Water. I like to think of them as operating at different 'speeds'.

The **Earth** signs are **Taurus**, **Virgo** and **Capricorn**. The Earth element is stable, grounded and concerned with practical matters. A Libra with a lot of Earth in their chart works best at a very slow, steady speed. (I refer to these in the text as 'Earthy'.)

The **Air** signs are **Gemini**, our friend **Libra** and **Aquarius** (who is the 'Water-carrier', *not* a Water sign). The Air element enjoys ideas, concepts and thoughts. It operates at a faster speed than Earth, not as fast as Fire but faster than Water and Earth. Imagine them as being medium speed.

The **Fire** signs are **Aries**, **Leo** and **Sagittarius**. The Fire element likes action, excitement and can be very impatient. Their speed is *very* fast. (I refer to these as Firey i.e. Fire-sign.)

The **Water** signs are **Cancer**, **Scorpio** and **Pisces**. The Water element involves feelings, impressions, hunches and intuition. They operate faster than Earth but not as fast as Air. A sort of slow-medium speed.

Chapter Three

The Ascendant

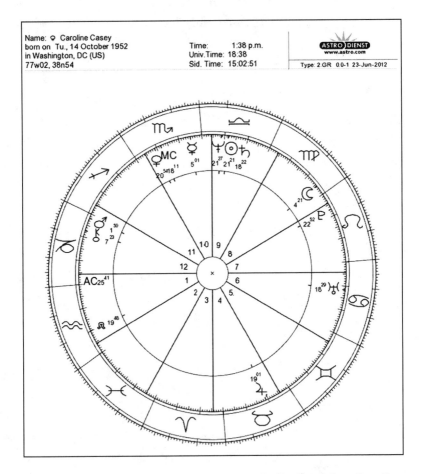

In this example chart above, I've used the data for Caroline Casey, a talented US astrologer. Look closely and you'll see the initials AC, at the quarter-to-nine position. That's the Ascendant and where a chart 'starts'. It's determined by the time and location of birth.

If you imagine the centre of the circle is the Earth, the map of the heavens is as if you were looking up from the Earth at the sky on that birth day.

The reason it's a circle is because the Earth is surrounded by the cosmos, so the outside part of the chart, which has the signs of the Zodiac on it, represents the cosmos, and the inner bit is the Earth.

The Ascendant is the part of the sky that was rising in the eastern horizon on the day of birth and changes every 2 hours into the next sign. If Caroline had been born 2 hours later, she'd have an Aquarius Ascendant.

If your Libra was born around 4am–6am in a country above the equator, their rising sign or Ascendant would most likely also be Libra...but if they were born a few hours later, their Ascendant would be the next sign on (which is Scorpio) and so on round the Zodiac.

Having a correct birth time is important because if your chart starts in the wrong sign, all the houses (which we'll learn about in Chapter Five) will also be in the wrong place.

If you don't know your Libra's time of birth, ignore this chapter.

And if you can't get your head around these ideas, don't worry; it will all make sense soon.

The Ascendant in Astrology is how you tackle life, the specs you wear, and how others see you. Because it's represented by your time of birth, it is therefore quite important. That moment of birth is unique to you and unless someone was born at the same time, in exactly the same place, his or her chart would be different. So when we say 'All Librans love beauty', we have to modify that statement by the rising sign or Ascendant and equally by the other parts of a chart, which we'll come onto in the next chapter.

I think of the Ascendant as being someone's kneejerk reaction. If they were under stress or put on the spot, their Ascendant sign would be more evident than their Sun sign...and ladies, if you're dating someone, their Ascendant will be the bit that strikes you in the first few minutes of meeting them. I can't tell you the amount of charts I've made for people who just couldn't understand how or why they ended up with the person they're with...until we do both of their charts and find that their Ascendant signs were compatible.

I'll give you a little example.

Queen Elizabeth II of England has a Capricorn Ascendant, Sun in Taurus and Moon in Leo. Her husband of over 64 years of marriage also has a Capricorn Ascendant, Sun in Gemini and...guess what? Moon in Leo too. So it's hardly surprising that even though their Sun signs aren't especially compatible (she's an Earth sign, he's an Air sign), their combined Moons and Ascendants help make their marriage more manageable.

Here are the various different Ascendants and what they're like for a Libra. I've also included little quotes from famous Libran people who actually have those Ascendants.

Aries Ascendant

'Just go out there and do what you have to do.' Martina Navratilova

As the first sign of the Zodiac and ruled by Mars the God of War, Aries likes to lead and be upfront where the action is. It is also a Fire sign, so the energy is swift and quick. They'll battle for what they think is right...and as it is the opposite sign to the Libra Sun, will catch themselves occasionally having active, fighting thoughts.

Taurus Ascendant

'You can't be a movie star when you're doing your laundry or when you're getting your food at the local grocery store.' Sigourney Weaver

This is the sign of slow, steady progress. You can't hurry them, and they prefer a stable, firm foundation to any plans. As Earth is slower than all the other elements, there is time to get the practical things in life sorted first before all the fluffy things happen. Don't be late with meals or you'll upset them!

Gemini Ascendant

'I don't like living alone, so it's nice if someone is there with me. I don't like travelling alone, being alone, eating alone, doing anything alone. I have never lived on my own and there's always been someone with me, either fellow musicians or friends.' Cliff Richard

Ruled by Mercury the God of Conversation and Communication, Gemini Asc likes nothing more than having a good chat, or 'debate' about Life, The Universe...and Everything. They'll also want to be up on the latest news, films and entertainment and are happiest surrounded by interesting company.

Cancer Ascendant

'The most sophisticated people I know – inside they are all children.' Jim Henson

Cancer is the sign of nurturing, Mum/Mom, home-cooked cosiness and emotional honesty. They love to be snuggled up in soft clothes, hugging the family pet, warm in the embrace of the family. Their view of the world is seen through the emotional haze of everyone-really-caring-and-empathising-with-each-other's-feelings-forever-and-ever.

Leo Ascendant

'That's what I am: an entertainer.' Britt Ekland

The Leo Asc gives the Libra Sun a jolly good excuse to show off. Ignore them at your peril. On a good day their warm Fire side will enjoy praise and adoration. Red carpets and individual, personal treatment will go down very well. Pointing out that someone else is smarter, more clever, more talented or beautiful won't, so avoid crushing comments if you want to stay friends.

Virgo Ascendant

'Some people regard discipline as a chore. For me, it is a kind of order

that sets me free to fly.' Julie Andrews

If you can ignore their general worrisome nature, Virgo Asc will carefully and diligently ensure every box is ticked, every smallest thought has been considered. If you can also keep up with the health issues, you're onto a winner. If you want everything in its place and a place for everything, Virgo Asc will provide it every time.

Libra Ascendant

'Always aim at complete harmony of thought and word and deed. Always aim at purifying your thoughts and everything will be well.' Mohandas (Mahatma) Gandhi

To have a Libra Sun and Asc doubles the fun. Fairness, balance, harmony and grace are constant aspirations. Whether they can be managed in this lifetime is possible but not always probable unless they're aiming for beatification. What is definite is this is the Asc that wants to weigh up every thought and action against that ideal.

Scorpio Ascendant

'I always cheer up immensely if an attack is particularly wounding because I think, well, if they attack one personally, it means they have not a single political argument left.' Margaret Thatcher

Not an Asc to trifle with. They are playing life-and-death stakes and winner takes all. Scorpio Asc demands trust and emotional sincerity so forget about bluff or woolly/wobbly thinking. They won't warm quickly, if at all, but they will respect emotional honesty and truth regardless of the pain levels.

Sagittarius Ascendant

'With the morn we mount and ride. Pilgrims of summer. The swift is our guide.' Marc Bolan

Let's get on a bus or a train or fly to some foreign far-off place on a Fire sign whim. Sagittarius Asc allows a Libra to venture into expansive territory, cranking up the Jupiter-ruled belief and jollity. One long party with everyone invited makes them happy and, provided their excesses aren't excessive, they will magically excite any bystanders.

Capricorn Ascendant

'Your children need your presence more than your presents.' Jesse Jackson

Of all the signs, Capricorn is the most serious and most reliable...mostly. They enjoy responsibilities and won't shirk from good old-fashioned hard work. Provided other chart factors are favourable, this Asc will lead the Libra into a sensible outlook on life, one that will take into account the fragility of human nature.

Aquarius Ascendant

'Let us learn to show our friendship for a man when he is alive and not after he is dead.' F. Scott Fitzgerald

'Be my friend, my deeply faithful friend' is the call-sign of Aquarius Asc and one that Libra is very happy to own as it's also an Air sign, which so enjoys thoughts and wacky discussions. The more, the merrier. Freedom is also written high in their world, so keep any restraining ideas firmly aside and let cool calmness rule.

Pisces Ascendant

'Meditation has only one reason: to get in touch with your soul, and then go beyond that and get in touch with the consciousness that your soul is a ripple of.' Deepak Chopra

Pisces is the last sign of the Zodiac and one that contains teeny bits of all the other signs, all mashed together sensitively. Fairies, angels and dolphins dusted with stars and twinkly bits – all this makes them seem shallow when in fact they're deeper than any sea. Pisces Asc will make a Libra touch twin-souls on a good day, and miss the bus due to daydreaming on a bad day!

Chapter Four

The Moon

If the Sun in Astrology represents our ego and our 'self', the Moon represents our inner self, and just like the Moon (in real life) reflects the light from the Sun, so the Moon in Astrology is our inner reflection.

It also represents our emotional self. So the Sun is the rational, ego, energy self and the Moon is the softer, emotional, feeling self.

All of this is fine if we're just doing Sun-sign Astrology, but if we're making up someone's chart, which will have not just the Ascendant, Sun and Moon but eight other planets, then there are an awful lot of things to think about.

Luckily we don't have to do that in this book. We're just getting the basics of Astrology, enough to answer a few life questions, and maybe just enough to help us understand the Libra in your life.

If your Libra has a Moon sign which is different to their Sun sign (which is more than likely as the Moon changes sign every 2 days), then one part of them, their rational part, might be at odds with their emotional self, and as Libra already has a problem making decisions, having a few more things to consider can create a nice meltdown.

So, it's important to understand your Libran's Moon sign, as that will more likely be expressed when they're having a bad, moody or grumpy time.

The same applies to you.

If, for instance, you're a Virgo and you've got Moon in Aquarius, one part of you is happy being careful and particular while the other more hidden side of you wants to be free and weirdly utopian. These parts might not gel very well, so making allowances for these two totally different energies in your psyche will make you feel less anxious.

The Dr Bach Flower Essences

In 1933 Dr Edward Bach, a medical doctor and Homeopath, published a little booklet called *The Twelve Healers and Other Remedies*. He was also, interestingly enough, a lovely Libra with Moon in Leo.

His theory was that if the emotional component a person was suffering from was removed, their 'illness' would also disappear. I tend to agree with this kind of thinking as most illnesses (except being hit by a bus) are preceded by an unhappy event or an emotional disruption that then sets into place the body getting out of sync.

Removing the emotional issue and bringing a bit of stability into someone's life, when they are having a hard time, can improve their overall health so much that wellness resumes.

Knowing which Bach Flower Essence can help certain worries and upsetments gives you and your Libran more control over your lives. I recommend the Essences a lot in my practice if I feel a certain part of a person's chart is under stress...and usually it's the Moon that needs help. The Essences describe the negative aspects of the character, which are focused on during treatment. This awareness helps reverse those trends, so when our emotional selves are nice and comfortable, we can then face each day with more strength.

I've quoted Dr Bach's actual words for each sign.

To use the Essences take 2 drops from the stock bottle and put them into a glass of water and sip. I tend to recommend putting them into a small water bottle, and sipping them throughout the day, at least 4 times. For young children, do the same.

Remember to seek medical attention if symptoms don't get better and/or seek professional counselling.

Aries Moon

'Style is knowing who you are, what you want to say, and not giving a damn.' Gore Vidal

When the Moon goes into Aries, things speed up, with fast and furious emotions, which can be difficult for the Libra Sun. On the positive side, they won't hold a grudge and once they've got 'whatever' out of their system, they're back to normal. The trick is to remember balance is Libra's call-sign and Aries' is action, so getting the two things to gel can be a challenge.

Bach Flower Essence Impatiens: *'Those who are quick in thought and action and who wish all things to be done without hesitation or delay.'*

Taurus Moon

'I never do any television without chocolate. That's my motto and I live by it. Quite often I write the scripts and I make sure there are chocolate scenes. Actually I'm a bit of a chocolate tart and will eat anything. It's amazing I'm so slim.' Dawn French

To feel comfortable, the Taurus Moon needs to have all the physical, practical things in life sorted out first, before they can do anything fluffy. They also like good sex, chocolate, good wine, tactile contact, silk, satin...you get the picture. They prefer a settled, secure environment and hate lots of change, just for the sake of it.

Bach Flower Essence Gentian: *'Those who are easily discouraged. They may be progressing well in the affairs of their daily life, but any small delay or hindrance to progress causes doubt and soon disheartens them.'*

Gemini Moon

'I have to live with both my selves as best I may.' Brigitte Bardot

As an Air sign, the Gemini Moon wants to communicate in an airy way, so feelings are processed mentally rather than emotionally. They are light, fluffy and constantly changing. For a

Libra, this makes things rather busy as the Sun will be weighing things up, and the Moon will be alternating between each twin. They feel better making short journeys, chatting and writing journals.

Bach Flower Essence Cerato: *'Those who have not sufficient confidence in themselves to make their own decisions.'*

Cancer Moon

'There is always one moment in childhood when the door opens and lets the future in.' Graham Greene

The Moon is 'at home' in the sign of Cancer and holds onto feelings…almost forever. They will love snugly, soft cuddly pets/animals/babies and also cooking family meals and being united in that family unit. As this is a Water sign, it's a different energy from Libra, hence there might be some confusion between Libra's rational approach and Cancer's emotionality.

Bach Flower Essence Clematis: *'Living in the hopes of happier times, when their ideals may come true.'*

Leo Moon

'Nothing is so contagious as enthusiasm.' Samuel Taylor Coleridge

Do NOT ignore the Leo Moon. They want respect, attention, a few red carpets and people thanking them (profusely) for their magnanimity. If they're on your side, you have a friend for life who will lavish you with rewards, attention, sunbeams and happiness. They love more than anything to be adored, and feel comforted when their feelings are acknowledged.

Bach Flower Essence Vervain: *'Those with fixed principles and ideas, which they are confident are right.'*

Virgo Moon

'Health, Healing, Holy, Wholeness. They're all the same word.' Deepak Chopra

Virgo is the sign of health and healing and has the tendency to worry about...worrying. They like things clean and 'in place', and disorder of any sort sets them fretting. They are usually gentle souls who want nothing more than everything in its place. Purity and cleanliness are paramount, and health and healing high on their to-do lists.

Bach Flower Essence Centaury: *'Their good nature leads them to do more than their own share of work and they may neglect their own mission in life.'*

Libra Moon

'To me, love is when you meet that person and you think, "This is it; this is who I'm supposed to be with."' Kate Winslet

The Libra Sun loves relationship, and so does the Libra Moon, so this can produce a person who wants nothing more than to be in the 'perfect' relationship. Alas, we are just mortal human beings, so a certain amount of reality must be absorbed to make them more contented. It also ups the indecisiveness as they constantly want to make the 'right' choice and can end up not choosing at all because they're too busy deciding.

Bach Flower Essence Scleranthus: *'Those who suffer from being unable to decide between two things, first one seeming right then the other.'*

Scorpio Moon

'The point of power is always in the present moment.' Louise Hay

The Scorpio Moon is firmly fixed into wanting to trust they have the emotional power to withstand any emotional upsetment. They are focused and intent. Their X-ray eyes look deeply into your soul so you have to blink to stop the intrusion. Faithful and devoted to getting to the centre of deeply held beliefs, they can sense a lie at 50 paces.

Bach Flower Essence Chicory: *'They are continually correcting what they consider wrong and enjoy doing so.'*

Sagittarius Moon

'There is more wisdom in your body than in your deepest philosophy.'
Friedrich Nietzsche

Another Fire sign, the Sagittarius Moon loves to debate the higher planes of life, loves travelling literally and metaphorically, and equally will state things 'as they are'. They won't hold back from their personal convictions and enjoy foreign cultures, cooking and ideas. Ruled by benevolent Jupiter the God of Expansion, they also have a tendency to exaggerate.

This Essence comes under the heading 'Over-Sensitive to Influences and Ideas'.

Bach Flower Essence Agrimony: *'They hide their cares behind their humour and jesting and try to bear their trials with cheerfulness.'*

Capricorn Moon

'If you keep that impulsive, instinctive feeling even when you're being beaten down or exhausted or waylaid, you'll be successful.' Michael Douglas

One of the more severe Moon signs to have, they're jolly good at being self-critical and even a little hard on themselves. They enjoy challenges. Hate triviality. Prefer deep emotional experience and can withstand more let-downs than most due to an inner robust attitude.

Bach Flower Essence Mimulus: *'Fear of worldly things, illness, pain, accident, poverty, of dark, of being alone, of misfortune. They secretly bear their dread and do not speak freely of it to others.'*

Aquarius Moon

'I love everyone and everyone loves me. My apparent enemy becomes my friend, a golden link in the chain of my good.' Florence Scovel Shinn

The independent-thinking Aquarius Moon feels things differently from other signs. Friendship and altruism are top priority as are the state of the world/planet and community. Their feelings are less angst-ridden, more concerned with freedom and lack of restrictions. Ruled by wacky Uranus, also more likely to be individual and different.

Bach Flower Essence Water Violet: *'For those who like to be alone, very independent, capable and self-reliant. They are aloof and go their own way.'*

Pisces Moon

'You can take no credit for beauty at 16. But if you are beautiful at 60, it will be your soul's own doing.' Marie Stopes

This is the Moon of extreme sensitivity. Fairies, angels and long-lost soul-loves. Feelings are intuitive and on a bad day overwhelming. A more difficult Moon sign for a Libra because of the occasional ability to completely lose the plot. Gentle handling works best and all forms of spirituality are enjoyed. Life is not as it seems.

Bach Flower Essence Rock Rose: *'For cases where there even appears no hope or when the person is very frightened or terrified.'*

Chapter Five

The Houses

I think it must be because I'm a Pisces and very imaginative that I've never had a problem understanding what a house is. The same cannot be said for everyone, so I hope in this little explanation, things might become a little clearer.

If we imagine that the centre of the birth chart is the Earth spinning in space, the Ascendant, which we discussed earlier, is the horizon, looking out into the distance in the east (if you live in the western hemisphere). If we draw a line across the chart from that point, that represents the time of birth and when it gets to the other side of the circle, it reaches a point we call the 7th house. This is because if you divide a circle into 12, the bit opposite our starting point at the Ascendant (called the Descendant) will be the 7th section.

Early astrologers called the houses 'Mansions' as these were the places that the planets 'lived' in the chart. I use the Equal House system, which is the most ancient system, so all of my houses are the same size. Most computer programmes and websites use a system called Placidus, which wasn't introduced into England until the 18th century and makes each house a different size, and is too confusing for a beginner.

We divide the circle anti-clockwise, or as they say in the USA counter-clockwise.

The signs of the Zodiac are how we divide the heavens; they don't have anything to do with the constellations.

I got into a dreadful flap the day before I was due to give an Astrology talk to a friendly group in Glastonbury. I was gaily demonstrating my home-made flip chart map of the world/heavens to my lovely husband, and was telling him that having his Sun in the 8th meant he was more intense than other Taureans, when he asked, quite innocently, *why* each house had a meaning.

DOH!

I gave him the astrological answer, but that wasn't good enough; he wanted to know the scientific reason…which is of course: there isn't one.

Astrology uses astronomical principles but they are not the same.

Astronomy is about where the planets are, what they do, how old they are, the orbits they have, all the other 'things' in space including black holes, constellations, stars, planets, comets and asteroids. My dictionary defines it as the 'science of the heavenly bodies'.

Astrology is about how those planets and the Sun (which is a star) relate to us human beings on Earth, taking into account that we're all living in the same space. We're not separate from them. My dictionary defines it as the 'study of planetary movements etc. regarded as an influence on human affairs'.

So astronomers don't talk about Venus reflecting love and affection. They talk about its depth/width/size/orbit/surface area and lots of other mathematical stuff…all very dry.

Where the Sun is located in the chart is determined by the time of birth. The further into the day you were born, the further round the circle your Sun will fall. If your Libra was born round about lunch-time, their Sun (the little circle with the dot in the middle) would be in the highest position in the chart round about houses 9/10.

Your Libra is still a Libra. Still concerned with beauty and fairness, but the location of the Sun modifies that expression. Someone with Sun in the 7th is quite different to someone with Sun in the 4th.

I admit, it's a small difference but it's one that keeps astrologers on their toes and as far as I'm concerned makes the subject come alive for me.

Would a Libra with Sun in the 1st be more likely to bop you on the head if you were rude than someone with Sun in the 12th?

In *How to Read Your Astrological Chart* (a wonderful book all Astrology students should read) Donna Cunningham says: 'If the intermediate cusps were real divisions rather than artificial ones, there wouldn't be such a controversy about them.'[13]

Quite right. There is no obvious reason why each house *means* something until you start comparing people's charts and immersing yourself in the subject.

As this is only a teeny book and I don't have space to explain or demonstrate in any great detail, just take my word for it that each house has a meaning, and all you need to know for the moment is which meaning fits your Libran the best.

I'm only going to give you the interpretations for where the Sun falls in the chart, not where the Moon might be, otherwise this book will cost twice as much, so you'll have to use the astro.com website (or get in touch with me) if you need to know more.

Here are the 12 houses, and what is means for the Sun to be in each house. If you make your Libran's chart correctly, that ☉ symbol will be in one of those divisions. In our example charts of Marc and Caroline, their Suns are in the 11th and 9th respectively.

These examples below, again, are all of real people whose birth times we know, so we can be sure that they have the given characteristics.

I've also included what sign the Ascendant will be, as that will change as the Sun travels round the circle.

The First House: House of Personality

'I am a bit of a spiritual anarchist. I am very sort of, in your face. I'm not for the institutions. I'm pro the individual. I don't care much for bullshit.' Stuart Wilde

This is where the chart starts, so if your Libran has their Sun located here, they're going to be more 'in your face', more active, alert and on the ball than someone whose Sun is in a later house. They enjoy being upfront about things and are quick to make judgements and decisions. A more assertive placement.

(Ascendant Libra or Virgo)

The Second House: House of Money, Material Possessions and Self-Worth

'I can resist everything except temptation.' Oscar Wilde

The 2nd house is where the Libra Sun slows down a little and wants to smell the roses. They like good wine, fine food and a healthy bank balance. Chocolate appeals, as does a healthy sex life. Life will be more practically based and they love tactile, physical contact. They prefer to be financially secure, so can worry a little about money, but equally their view of life is resourceful and practical.

(Ascendant Virgo or Leo)

The Third House: House of Communication and Short Journeys

'I've always been good at change. I mean my life has always been about change. I did 11 years as a columnist at the Mirror. *I did 11 years of* Points of View.*'* Anne Robinson

Like our 3rd sign friend Gemini, Sun in the 3rd house wants to zip around, being connected, mobile at the ready, flitting from here to here. They might move house a lot, or change locations, and on top of the list will be variety and diversity. They also feel a lot better having some form of transport, be it a bike, motor scooter, car or, if they're rich enough, personal chauffeur.

(Ascendant Leo or Cancer)

The Fourth House: House of Home, Family and Roots

'I always wanted my music to influence the life you were living emotionally – with your family, your lover, your wife, and, at a certain

point, with your children.' Bruce Springsteen

The Libra Sun in the 4th house is concerned with the family and all things domestic and cuddle-able. They might own lots of pets or cuddly toys, or never want to leave home and feel happiest with only close relatives. Their home will have made a big impression on them in their childhood, for good or bad, and they can be a little sentimental.

(Ascendant Cancer or Gemini)

The Fifth House: House of Creativity and Romance

'This Spirit that has created all traditional forms and must ever create new ones.' Edith Stein

This is the house that wants to create, be it art, music or dance or equally creating lots of babies. They enjoy being admired, respected and adored. Romance features highly and they may fall in love with love itself. They are happiest 'making' things, be it drama, stories or a fuss!

(Ascendant Gemini or Taurus)

The Sixth House: House of Work and Health

'To be a conscious parent, and really look to that little being's mental and physical health is a responsibility.' John Lennon

The 6th house governs our work and health, so can make the native more concerned with health issues, be it their own or that of others close to them. They will also work better when things are organised and in place. Messiness won't work here. They love order and things arranged in a certain way.

(Ascendant Taurus or Aries)

The Seventh House: House of Relationships and Marriage

'The ideal of fair and balanced harmony between people is admittedly attractive to me.' Stephen Arroyo

For any clients I work with who have their Sun here, I always 'prescribe' a close personal relationship as they feel empty and only half a person without someone else to reflect their ideas and support them. As this is similar to the 7th sign, which is Libra, a person with Sun here likes to share themselves. The only possible drawback is they might get so influenced by their partner that they lose their own identity, so it's a tricky balance between independence and union.

(Ascendant Aries or Pisces)

The Eighth House: House of Life Force in Birth, Sex, Death and After-Life

'If I'm going to Hell, I'm going there playing the piano.' Jerry Lee Lewis

As this is one of the more intense houses in the birth chart, having the Libra Sun here will make for someone who is more focused and possibly deeply passionate. They might not be passionate about love itself, but they will have deep feelings for their favourite interest.

(Ascendant Pisces or Aquarius)

The Ninth House: House of Philosophy and Long-Distance Travel

'I am filled with an abundant enthusiasm for my heroic journey. Open my path before me and grant me the opportunity to be of maximum good in the world.' Caroline W. Casey

Exploring foreign countries and far-off places, if only in magazines, not in the flesh, will keep the 9th house Sun eternally happy. Further education and long-distance travel are assured, as is the desire to be inspired by other cultures.

(Ascendant Aquarius or Capricorn)

The Tenth House: House of Social Identity and Career

'Music is something I must do, business is something I need to do, and Africa is something I have to do. That's the way it breaks down in my life.' Bob Geldof

This is the highest place that the Sun can be in a chart, so therefore if the Libra Sun is here, they are more likely to want to succeed in what they do, and second best just won't do. Ambition can drive them, and meaningful work is a must.

(Ascendant Capricorn or Sagittarius)

The Eleventh House: House of Social Life and Friendships

'Friendship entails a paradoxical blending of intimacy and individuality. Friends, unlike families, have no claim on each other to live in certain ways.' Thomas Moore

As this is the house of friendship and altruism, the Libra Sun here will incline someone towards spending time in groups and organisations with a benefit to 'mankind'. Maybe there is also a tendency to avoid closeness and to be slightly more cool in relationships as there is a necessity to feel free to 'be'. They enjoy working with others, and being a small cog in a big wheel. More likely also to want to 'save the world'.

(Ascendant Sagittarius or Scorpio)

The Twelfth House: House of Spirituality

'Each one has to find his peace from within. And peace to be real must be unaffected by outside circumstances.' Mohandas (Mahatma) Gandhi

This is the house that demands protection and time away from life's hurts and rawness. They need time alone to meditate, time for contemplation and at the very least a special place to retire to, even if it's only the shower and lots of water. If they were in a band they'd be the backing vocalist, not the lead singer. They like to take the back seat in organisations and work best from a place of seclusion.

(Ascendant Scorpio or Libra)

Chapter Six

The Difficulties

I agree with Libran Thomas Moore when he talks in his *Care of the Soul* about the subject of love:

> Many of the problems people bring to therapy involve the high expectations and the rock-bottom experiences of love. It is clear that love is never simple, that it brings with it struggles of the past and hopes for the future, and that it is loaded with material that may be remotely – if at all – connected to the person who is the apparent object of love.[14]

My clients rarely make an appointment to share with me how lovely their partner is, and how wonderful their life is together. Maybe it is unrealistic to expect love to unite everyone and for it all to be happy-ever-after, but equally I think it's important not to forget what you're striving for.

This is represented by the glyph of Libra = the scales. While they are operating well, and everything is being evaluated alongside their expectations, all is well. But once the balancing act gets complex, Librans will wobble almost as much as a Pisces. I said 'almost', as Pisces is the worst for the wobbles.

One of the biggest difficulties for any Libra is making up their mind. It's almost as if they become two people while the soul searching is going on. There's not a lot you can do to help, other than supporting their decision-making process. Remember, don't rush them; it will only make things worse.

I've included the few genuine questions that I get asked in my private practice and the sort of answers or suggestions that I might give.

My Libra doesn't know if he/she wants to get married this year or next, and where we should live after we get married and what job he/she should have.

This is a constant dilemma for a Libra. All those things to think about and 'get straight' in their head. The worry is they'll make the wrong decisions and will live with the consequences and regrets.

If we think a little like Eckhart Tolle guides us to do in *The Power of Now*, it's best to:

a) Just tackle one thing at a time and
b) Not think too far ahead.

Rather than worrying about all the things that come *after* the marriage, it would be best for this person to concentrate on the marriage itself. You can do the delaying tactic that you won't even discuss the place to live or the job until *after* the wedding.

Then get on with all the plans necessary to make the wedding as smooth as possible.

My Libra hates their job but doesn't want to leave it because it pays well.

I know so many Libra people that have more than one job. It's quite uncanny. They might be a mum and a therapist, or have lots of little part-time jobs, or work in one place, then pull away and work somewhere else. This tends to be because of the old adage that the 'grass is always greener'. For this dilemma, it's no good even thinking about changing a job, if they haven't made plans to find a new one!

If they send their CV out to a few employers and get some feedback, they might find that the job they're in is better...or not. But nothing will happen if all they do is complain about the job they're in.

Unless you're self-employed, all jobs can become tedious.

What's better is to think whether or not your Libran's current job gels with their deepest motivations, mindset and ideals. Working for an employer who uses child labour, or doesn't train staff, or bends the rules (a big no-no for a Libra!) or is breaking the law in surreptitious ways will make your Libra feel ill, so my suggestion would be to change jobs ASAP.

My Libra says I don't love her/him the right way.
This is a very sad situation for a Libra. Love is such an all-encompassing entity, for it to feel wrong for a Libra makes living with them a terrible state, as all they will do is criticise your every action/thought/suggestion.

A young lady called Cher emailed me about her plight. She is in her thirties, living with her partner, and has one child, a Libra son. She is qualified in naturopathic medicine. I asked her how she would *like* to be loved and she replied:

'How would I like to be loved? This is the heart of my sadness right now, as I don't feel that my partner loves me in a way that I crave. I want to be loved honestly and passionately. I want to be consumed by it. I feel incomplete when I am a single woman even though I know that I am happier that way, as I don't make compromises just to stay in a relationship. I want to be told in words that reach my heart about how I am seen and understood, valued and treasured. I want to feel a heart connection. I'm not interested in flowers or chocolates. I crave risky and sometimes hurtful loving. I am living without feeling love for my partner for what seems like years, and I have slowly dried up and lost my passion; I have become cynical and bitter. I want love to come crashing into my life and to illuminate me and re-ignite my passion for life.'

As this particular lady gave me her birth data, we can have a little look at some suggestions for her predicament.

She has a Gemini Ascendant, so she needs to be in a

changeable environment, surrounded by interesting people, and would enjoy short, daily journeys. My mother, who I mentioned in my book *How to Bond with an Aquarius*, also has a Gemini Ascendant and even though she never learned to drive she went out every day, walking, cycling, getting a lift from a friend, by taxi or using the Underground (subway, Metro).

Cher has her Sun in the 4th house, so probably needs to work from home; and if she's going to do that, and because she is a Libra, she will need to make sure her surroundings are beautiful and orderly. Please note I am not making any suggestions about her relationship, as that isn't the true issue. It's difficult for love to come to you – any sort of love – if you're feeling bitter and twisted. So first of all we need to make sure that she is happy and contented in her surroundings and life situation before we can tackle the relationship.

'I procrastinate, because I have a fear of being wrong, even to the point of having far too many emails in my account because I'm not sure if I should delete them or not. Likewise with clutter in my house, I might need or want that "thing" at some point, even though living among the physical clutter makes me stressed and depressed. Letting go of things is even harder now that I have a son – I want to hold on to every memory, and feel sad if I get rid of something that he has created or loved. I want to live in a clutter-free house! Yet I am drowning in clutter.'

I'd suggest a good old clear-out of old feelings and rubbish and not to worry about throwing out things that might be important. I think also the enormity of the task is making it seem worse than it actually is. An hour a day spent clearing clutter would be better, and less painful, than having a great splurge. She would also benefit from actually defining for herself what clutter is for her.

Is it lots of plastic bags, or her child's toys, or magazines or newspapers lying around, or boxes filled with things she'll never use?

Once she's worked out what her version of clutter is (because it's different for different people), she can get rid of it.

It might also help to write a little plan and keep it somewhere prominent, to remind her of what she's doing and why she's doing it. She's not clearing clutter; she's freeing herself from feeling boxed in.

I do think though that becoming a mother does involve a certain amount of extra stuff. All those things that belong to the child, like buggies, wellies, coats and clothes and books and toys and the things that kiddies like to play with when they're small do build up. When they get to be older, all those things miraculously disappear. I think it's hard to be 'Zen' when you've got little ones, so it might be more practical and less stressful to accept that with motherhood comes stuff. When my son was little, I showed him how to tidy up. I didn't *tell* him to tidy; we did it together.

Librans like to do things with other people rather than on their own, and 'team work' works well with little Librans, so Cher could get her son to help her a little every day.

Her Moon is in the sign of Scorpio and, as we have already discovered, Scorpio is an intense, emotional energy. She wants to feel passion. She even mentions that she craves 'risky and hurtful loving'. I'm not so sure that getting involved in love that is *risky* and *hurtful* will be appealing to her Libra Sun. This is something that her Moon craves, so we have to find a way to satisfy her Moon but also keep her Sun sign happy.

It's necessary to balance her needs with those of her child, and risky loving isn't something that sits well with being a mum/mom. Maybe she can promise herself some of this when her child is grown up or maybe she could spend a small amount of time doing something a bit more risky like learning how to sky-dive or parachuting for charity. It's important to balance motherhood with passion – not impossible, but maybe a bit more challenging. She could easily get a babysitter to look after her son for the weekend. Then she and her partner could spend a weekend away somewhere remote and 'natural' like the north coast, somewhere windswept and beautiful to fill up her inner-beauty reserves.

Chapter Seven

The Solutions

'And even should we not love each other from the bottom of our hearts – must we then have a grudge against each other if we do not love each other perfectly?' Friedrich Nietzsche (Scorpio Ascendant, Sun in 11th, Moon in Sagittarius)

I hope you're getting a bit more of a feel about what a Libra likes and how to love one, as that is their raison d'être. In this chapter we'll be discussing what tactics to take if your Libra needs *more* loving. You'll know when they're feeling out of sorts because they'll come back with smart replies, or cutting comments. They won't be rude or violent (Librans rarely are) but they'll be grumpy and argumentative.

You'll know if your Libra is seriously under-loved when they won't even argue with you, and just act passively. This is a very sad situation for a Libra. Love is so important to a Libra for it to feel wrong makes living with them terribly hard.

Celia helpfully lets us know exactly what are important things for her to feel loved:

'Kindness, thoughtfulness – remembering birthdays, buying little things for each other randomly just to show you care, making or doing something to help without being nagged into it. Bonding of the home being important to both, not set tasks for each. Keeping in touch regularly, even a few words in a text or a postcard so you are together in spirit. Knowing when the other one is not feeling too good and genuinely caring and trying to help in some way. Little compliments and praise for things. Functioning as a close, loving, warm unit with a mutual support network, yet being an individual within that unit.'

Jacqueline, who is a media support manager for a New York

publisher and part-time yoga teacher, tells us how she likes to be loved:

> 'Without judgement – exactly the way my husband loves me. He loves me with patience and understanding. Regardless of my flaws or temper or type A personality or occasional attitude. It is great to be loved by someone who always sees the good in you no matter what.'

Remember the Flower Essences I mentioned in Chapter Four; they work a treat during wobbly moments.

Aries Asc or Moon

Do something physical with your Libra. Take them out of the house, somewhere where they can bash a ball, or run around, or get those feelings out of their system without bopping you on the head. A round of golf, a tennis match, a few hours swimming, a game of squash, rounders or basketball – something competitive but nothing that is going to get you in the firing line so don't go shooting...Aries is all about the body and energy, so something energetic is best. They can then thrash out their feelings on the green, court or pool and you can 'be' there for them while that happens.

Taurus Asc or Moon

Get the kettle on and some nice, low-fat cakes organised. Or go one better and take your Libra out for a nice meal. Somewhere beautiful with pretty surroundings, where the wallpaper matches the tablecloths, or the staff wear clean, smart uniforms. Don't even think about getting a take-away or going to McD's; that won't work while they're in this mindset. Take things slowly, don't rush them, and let them talk – or not.

Gemini Asc or Moon

You will need some form of transport to make a Libra/Gemini combo feel better. It's a fact that they feel better making some sort of short journey, some change of scene, so get them into the car and let them talk, talk, talk…until they haven't got anything left to say about the problem. When they start commenting on passers-by or the scenery, you know they're feeling a little better.

Cancer Asc or Moon

Invite your Libra/Cancer over for a home-cooked meal that you loving prepared yourself. It doesn't have to be cordon-bleu but it does have to be made with love by your own hands. Ignore any comments about how they might have done a better job themselves; this is just the grumpy bit getting an airing, so hold your tongue and let them relax into enjoying your company and being with someone who cares. If there are any small animals around, or little children they can fuss over, they will feel better.

Leo Asc or Moon

You're going to have to work a little harder to please a Libra who has Leo bits. Second best won't do. They want to feel exclusive attention from you and need a chance to let off steam. You can volunteer to help. 'What shall I do?' will go down well, but you might just find that they've got the solutions – they just want to act out how they feel about them. Prepare for major dramatics; this is a combination less likely to suffer quietly.

Virgo Asc or Moon

A wobbly Libra/Virgo needs quiet space and cool, calm surroundings. They will be worrying about their health, so any advice that Deepak Chopra suggests will be helpful, such as taking responsibility for feelings, feeling where they are in the body and what those sensations feel like, writing them down, releasing them with a ritual, then celebrating their release.

Thinking less always helps as all the Air signs think far too much. And do use Bach Flower Essence Centuary; it's a lifesaver for out-of-control worries.

Libra Asc or Moon

Be nice! A double Libra will be an indecisive wreck, and pointing that out won't help. Stay away from any decisions. Don't ask them what they want – in troubled times they can barely think – so make all the decisions about lunch, shopping, cooking and eating. Find something truly beautiful and share it with your double Libra. Point out some lovely things that are true, take them to see a beautiful sunset, take a walk through a pretty meadow or landscaped garden. If you don't have the time or the money, set their computer to have a picture of nature on their screen-saver. Listen to gentle music together. Just 'be'.

Scorpio Asc or Moon

You will need to be firm and centred with a Scorp/Libra. Being fluffy and soft won't work. If you think of colours like deep blood red and things like being stung by a scorpion you'll get the idea. They want to take drastic measures to make themselves feel better. This can involve throwing caution to the winds and doing something completely out of character, so I tend to suggest to Scorp/Libra clients to do things like write a letter to the people or problem concerned...and burn it...and watch the flames eat away the problem. Provided the intention is deep and meaningful, it will work just as well as drastic actions that will be later regretted.

Sagittarius Asc or Moon

As a Fire sign, the Sag/Libra will want to let off steam in an active, physical way. As they so love long-distance travel and philosophical pursuits, a quick trip away to a distant, exotic country works well, as does finding the 'meaning' to what is going on. Prepare to quote philosophical texts such as those by fellow Sag/Libra Nietzsche and immerse them in the 'bigger picture'. They won't want to think about teeny, unimportant things during a personal crisis, so don't remind them of petty things. Stay big.

Capricorn Asc or Moon

As this is a more serious combination, your Cap/Libra will enjoy wise words from an elder – someone older than them who has been there, done that very thing they're fretting about, and has got the tee-shirt. They like to think of serious, practical, traditional subjects that have meaning and, when they're in a head-spin, prefer and respond better to wise counsel. If you've got any elderly relatives, drag your Cap/Libra to see them, so they can actually 'see' everything-will-be-alright. To get to be old, you have to have taken some risks, so finding out how this older relative might have survived their own tragedies will inspire your Libra to better things.

Aquarius Asc or Moon

Anyone with Aquarius planets loves to do something weird and wacky every now and then. They won't follow the 'normal' life path and prefer to almost be the outsider, so if their life goes wobbly, don't expect to get them back on track with 'normal' solutions. One thing is for sure: they will want their friends to stand by them, and will enjoy the support of organisations or clubs or groups that they have an affinity for. In the short term, getting outside in the fresh air helps as Aquarius is an Air sign, so deep breathing and meditation make a difference.

Pisces Asc or Moon

The sign of the mystical and spiritual, Pisces/Libra will love the more esoteric solutions to problems, so you can use Angel cards and the Flower Essences to assist. Burn incense; suggest

Eurythmy (a form of healing movement developed by Rudolph Steiner, a Pisces). They also need time and space to reconfigure, as they're more likely to have picked up everyone else's feelings and angst which might have contributed to their present problems. Keeping a dream diary, or having hypnotherapy, also helps during wobbly phases.

Chapter Eight

Loving Tactics

As this little book was written to help you love a Libra, I will now go through the various different Librans you'll come across in real life, everyone from your child to your boss.

Each sign sits more happily in some placements than others. It's easier, say, to imagine the Libra characteristics in your lover than in your boss, but there will be people who have a Libra boss, so how do we make the best of that?

The qualities we've discussed that are typical of a Libra will come across in a different manner, say, in the workplace than in a romantic situation, so let's find out how to get along with this sign in all these different permutations.

Your Libra Child

I have a Libra child, so most of what I'm going to tell you is from personal experience.

Babydom is not a problem for Libra children. They don't have to think too much about things and most of the time their parents make the decisions. As they get older, more decisions have to be made and this is when the problems can start. Try not to give your Libran child too many alternatives.

This or that? Up or down? Black or blue? That's enough to keep them occupied for a while.

Here's Angela talking about her childhood;

'I'm so scared of making the wrong decision that I generally don't make one at all. I genuinely had no childhood dreams as I partly couldn't pick one thing and partly didn't like to presume/hope. Sadly, I'm still the same!'

Once decisions become bigger, it becomes more difficult for the Libra child. They want to cover every option. They won't want to just go with the most obvious choice. They want to weigh and muse, and think...until you're almost crazy with anticipation.

One Christmas my teen son and I went to choose some Christmas presents for my ex-in-laws. When I asked him what he wanted to get, he had no idea, but also he didn't want to go with any of my suggestions. I just wasn't helping. We walked around town, with him worrying about getting something nice on his small pocket money budget...until eventually he became tearful with the stress.

I found a nice scarf for his Nana, but his first reaction was 'It looks like something a soap actress would wear' (!) so in the end I said I'd accept any responsibility if the gift he bought wasn't liked.

I'd take the rap.

'I don't want to buy something just for the sake of it' was a continuing mantra, but equally he had to buy something, and that something was becoming more and more elusive as we wandered around from shop to shop.

What didn't help was the fact that he'd asked all the people concerned what they'd like and they all (unfortunately) had said, 'I don't want anything in particular; just get me a surprise.'

This is not helpful for a Libra. A surprise? Argh! What sort of a surprise? The thinking then starts to go into overdrive with all the possibilities until a state of sheer frozen nothingness is reached.

Small tip.

Don't give a Libra child too many alternatives. Just a few choices. Or at the very least, talk them through *how* you make a choice as you do it. Or suggest a few things that need to be achieved from *making* the decision.

Indecision is a nightmare state for a Libra, so don't let them get that far. It's not fun.

One thing that did work with my son was to ask him how he'd *feel* when he'd made the decision…and it's one you can use for younger Librans. Get them to focus on the *feeling* that they know they'll have, once the decision is made. They might feel relaxed, or at peace, or less stressed, or contented.

Whatever that feeling is, make sure they're focused on *that*, not on the anguish that deciding can do to them. They must focus on the outcome, not the difficulty.

This worked a treat once when son-and-heir was deliberating about what to 'do' when some products he'd ordered online hadn't arrived. He was upset because he thought the sender had had ample time for the items to arrive. Being a human being and part of the human race, I'm well aware that other people never do as much as you expect and the postal service in the UK is as good as possible, but not perfect.

So I asked him, 'How will you *feel* when it arrives?' and he gave me a little list. So I asked again, 'Talk me through what will happen when it arrives; imagine what will happen' and he told me that the doorbell would ring, and he'd have to go to the door and sign the little machine that the delivery person would have. He spent a few moments describing that scenario…then I left his room and went into the kitchen to make a cup of tea.

Less than five minutes later, the doorbell rang and, as I was busy, I asked him to answer the door…it was the deliveryman!

Now, I know that his *thinking* didn't make the delivery person arrive precisely at that moment. What I did demonstrate was that sometimes you can be 'in tune' with life, rather than struggling against it.

Your Libra Boss

I have friends who either have a Libra boss, or who are bosses themselves. Generally they're easy to get on with, as they hate to upset people.

Problems occur if they have to 'be' the boss and make people redundant, or sack them, or give them warnings. They hate doing things like this and will want to run a mile because of the fairness issue. They prefer it if the team work together and there is a certain amount of sharing in the job.

Bruce Springsteen, the singer-songwriter, got the nickname 'The Boss' when his band first formed and he took it upon himself to get the money for the band from the gigs they did.

In an interview in *Creem* in 1981 he had this to say about bosses:

> Well, the thing I have with this 'Boss' is funny because it came from people like that, who work around you. And then, somebody started to do it on the radio. I hate being called 'Boss.' (laughs) I just do. Always did from the beginning. I hate bosses. I hate being called the boss. It just started from all the people around me, then by somebody on the radio and once that happens, everybody said 'Hey Boss,' and I'd say, 'No. Bruce. BRUCE.' I always hated that. I always hated being called 'Boss.'[15]

So even though he is a boss in a way, or his own life, but not in isolation, there are a team of people that help him in his shows: he has to write the songs, perform them, keep this band motivated, go from city to city, go to the recording studio, be interviewed by the press; he is an amazingly resilient performer too.

In one year (2012) he scheduled 20 gigs in 24 days around the USA, then 33 gigs in 48 days around Europe. That's a lot of work, not just the gigging, but also the travelling from Spain, across Europe to Finland. I felt tired just reading the schedule.

So what's it like working for a Libra boss?

First of all, you will need to be well turned out. You won't last a minute working for a Libra if you don't look reasonably clean and tidy. You will have to be punctual, as I don't know any

Librans who are consistently late. You will also be expected to be all those things that Libras like, as in fair, balanced, non-confrontational and organised.

As Libra is an Air sign, you'll find your Libra boss will enjoy conversation, and any bright ideas you may have. They will expect pleases and thank-yous and a general level of politeness...obviously taking into account the culture and upbringing of the organisation you are in. Having a cool, calm demeanour will also score points.

Your (Female) Libra Lover

Your Libra lady will want to be treated...like a lady. If you're a rough and tumble sort, you'll find it hard to attract a Libra date, especially if you don't care about your appearance.

Here's Celia talking about her appearance:

'I always look in the mirror before going out but as I become older just a quick glance is sufficient! Up until I had children, looks and style were very important and I was lucky enough to be tall and slim; everything had to be colour co-ordinated and perfect and I could spend half an hour choosing a pair of earrings or a scarf.'

I've yet to meet a Libra that doesn't care how they look, so *you* must care a little about how you look if you want to be in this person's world for any length of time.

I've found the best way to understand what a Zodiac sign is looking for in a mate is to consult the dating websites...and I'll repeat what I've said in other books of mine, that most people are looking for an extension of themselves, because they know themselves the best.

I asked Heather how she'd like to be loved:

'I would like to be loved with caring; to be cherished; to be someone's No. 1; with tenderness; with passion.'

Linda is a 45-year-old lady who is looking for love. The way she describes herself and what she's looking for wouldn't alter one jot if she were younger or older. These are hard and fast Libran qualities.

First off, she describes things she likes, which is a nice intro as it gives you a fair idea of her interests:

'I love the smell of summer rain, to feel the wind on my face and swishing through the autumn leaves. I still get excited by thunderstorms and snow, heavy rain and jumping in puddles with my wellies on. My holidays these days mostly involve singing, dancing and sitting around a campfire with friends or walking in the beautiful British countryside. I care deeply about the planet and the natural world and strive to protect it and live simply and sustainably.'

As you can see, she knows a bit about her Sun sign and Ascendant (which is useful for my research purposes!):

'Being a typical Libran with the spark of Sagittarius rising I've had an interesting and adventurous life with plenty of travelling on all sorts of levels from sailing and skiing, backpacking around the world, to the more inner journeys of emotional and spiritual exploration. I'm slim, athletic and attractive, and can turn my hand to most things without being brilliant at anything. I tend to be a positive, optimistic initiator and have a strong sense of commitment in all that I do and in the relationships I have. I am content in my own company but also love to be with friends and would like to have that special person in my life to share the ups and downs of this wondrous adventure.'

She also mentions her work experience and background. Note the Sagittarius influence of education and the need to be outdoors; these are both strong Sagittarius essentials.

'After many years working in education, psychology and therapy, I started my own natural health business, which became all-consuming. I still spend far too much time on the computer and therefore welcome any distraction, whether it is a practical job to do, coffee with friends, or swimming and walking to keep fit. However, the business is now thriving so I can relax and focus more on achieving a better balance in my life.'

Hah! I had to laugh when she said she wanted 'a better balance'...*such* a Libra statement!

'Being a city dweller provides plenty of cultural pleasures such as going to the local arts cinema, theatre, live music, restaurants and a wide variety of meetings and gatherings. However, I also love being in the countryside, taking in the beautiful vast landscapes of Britain, walking in the hills, along the coast, by the river, in the woods, wherever the air is clear and nature thrives.'

Note also that she doesn't mention what she's looking for in her ideal partner, but one would have to presume that they have similar interests. So the ideal partner for this lady would like the outdoors, care about the planet, would have to be 'slim, athletic and attractive'. Note also how she uses the word 'beautiful' to describe the countryside, as opposed to exciting or breathtaking.

Your (Male) Libra Lover

In this example we have Grant who is age 35 and looking for a partner.

'In my quest to ask, if not answer, the world's big questions, I walk a road that leads to bookstores, cafés, university libraries and beaches. A fan of the "Quirky Alone" movement, and a Libran of multiplicities, I dream of a vegan family farm and natural building community, and opening my own cooperative center, with spaces for

performance, research, discussion, health & wellness, and a museum of peaceful resistance and beloved future visions. One of my questions I might ask you is "What is Love?" As much as it might be cuddling for hours, it's also using my heart to promote peace. Getting my hands dirty at the animal sanctuary farm. Showing my appreciation of friends through a well-cooked meal. Celebrating life by dancing the tango. Keeping a garden for food and green joy. Petting your cat. When I grow a garden just the way dad taught me, or persevere through adversity like my mom, I channel the love of my parents.

When I am vegan and work toward non-violence, I express my love of the planet. When I listen to your words and your body, disagree without fighting, and kiss you with all of me fully present, tender, playful, and happy, I share myself completely with you. I read the Monocle *magazine for cosmopolitan style and design. The women I go for are smart, fit, healthy and not afraid to make the first move.'*

Helpfully he then gives us a description of what he's looking for in his ideal woman.

'Your smile is infectious, your laugh spontaneous, your tears compassionate. Called by nature, you'll roll in wildflowers and kiss until sunset. You love your strong, healthy body, but realize that your mind is sexier, and keep it well exercised. Lifelong learning is a way of life for you. You're comfortable tending a garden in the afternoon and changing into that little black dress for dinner. You are open to diversity – people, ideas, food, places.

A natural storyteller, you might travel the country performing...or championing a cause. You remember people's names. If you had someone special to dance with, you might enter a competition. You are assertive with your ideals, but diplomatic in expressing them. Religion may not meet your needs; you explore philosophies and innate wisdom. Often the peacemaker, you don't hesitate to bring thoughtful discussion into a relationship. You see a better world in your mind's eye, and know that it's possible.

You'd rather dance than sit on the sidelines, walk in a protest than read the headlines. Most of all, you are authentic, and know you are only here once to make a difference. In love, you co-create a peaceful and happy haven for us to share. In love, we are a dynamic duo, lightening burdens, celebrating solutions, joined in our journey through life.'

I think he went slightly over-the-top in his description – sometimes people get a bit carried away with their writing style on the Internet – but the basics have been highlighted. He's looking for someone like himself. Who's non-violent, tender and thoughtful.

I asked Michael how he would like to be loved.

'I would like to be loved gently, kindly and with a warmth of heart. I would like to be loved for the person I am and not just my looks. I would like to be loved sincerely. I would like to be touched, held, stroked a lot...physical contact is important. Even if it is just a finger touching my hand. I would like to be loved soul-to-soul.'

Ladies, please note what they are NOT looking for is brash, noisy, OTT or argumentative mates.

What to Do If Your Libra Relationship Ends
Fire sign

If you are a Fire sign – Aries, Leo or Sagittarius – you will need something active and exciting to help you get over your relationship ending.

You will also need to use the element of Fire in your healing process.

Get a nice night-light candle and light it and recite: 'I ... (your

name) do let you ... (Libran's name) go, in freedom and with love
so that I am free to attract my true soul-love.'

Leave the night light in a safe place to completely burn away.
Allow at least an hour. In the meantime gather up any
belongings or possessions that are your now ex-lover's and
deliver them back to your Libra. It's polite to telephone first and
notify your ex when you will be arriving.

If you have any photos of you together or other mementos or
even gifts, don't be in a rush to destroy them, as some Fire signs
are prone to do. Better to put them away in a box in the attic or
garage until you feel a little less upset.

In a few months' time, go through the box and keep the things
you like and give away the things you don't.

Earth sign

If you are an Earth sign – Taurus, Virgo or Capricorn – you will
feel less inclined to do something dramatic or outrageous. It
might also take you slightly longer to recover your equilibrium,
so allow yourself a few weeks and a maximum of three months
to grieve.

You will be using the Earth element to help your healing,
which can be expressed by using crystals.

The best crystals to use are the ones associated with your Sun
sign and also with protection.

Taurus = Emerald
Virgo = Agate
Capricorn = Onyx

Cleanse your crystal in fresh running water. Wrap it in some
pretty silk fabric, and then go on a walk into the countryside.
When you find a suitable spot that is quiet and where you won't
be disturbed, dig a small hole and place your crystal in the
ground.

Spend a few minutes thinking about your relationship, the good times and the bad. Forgive yourself for any mistakes you may have made.

Imagine a beautiful plant growing from the ground where you have buried your crystal, and the plant blossoming and growing strong.

This will represent your new love that will be with you when the time is right.

Air sign

If you're an Air sign – Gemini, Libra or Aquarius – you might want to talk about what happened first, before you finish the relationship. Air signs need reasons and answers, and can waste precious life-energy looking for those answers. You might need to meet with your Libran to tell him/her exactly what you think/thought about his/her opinions, ideas and thoughts. You might also be tempted to tell him/her what you think about them now, which I do not recommend.

Far better to put those thoughts into a tangible form by writing your ex-Libran a letter. It is not a letter that you are actually going to post, but you are going to put as much energy into writing it *as if* you were actually going to send it.

Write to them thus: 'Dear Libra, I expect you will be happy now in your new life, but there are a few things I would like to know and understand before I say goodbye.'

Then list all the annoying, aggravating, upsetting ideas that your (now ex) Libran indulged in. Make a list as long as you like. Put in as much detail as you feel comfortable with, including things like how many times they couldn't commit to your ideas or wavered about things. Keep writing till you can write no more, then end your letter with something like: 'Even though we were not suited, and I suffered because of this, I wish you well on your path.' Or some other positive comment.

Then tear your letter into teeny little pieces and put them into a small container. We are now going to use the element of Air to rectify the situation.

Take a trip to somewhere windy and high, like the top of a hill, and when you're ready, open your container and sprinkle a few random pieces of your letter into the wind. Don't use the entire letter or you run the risk of littering, just enough pieces to be significant.

Watch those little pieces of paper fly into the distance and imagine them connecting with the nature spirits.

Your relationship has now ended.

Water sign

If you are a Water sign – Cancer, Scorpio or Pisces – you might find it more difficult to recover quickly from your relationship. You might find yourself weeping at inopportune moments, or when you hear 'your' song on the radio, or when you see other couples happily being in each other's company. You might lie awake at night worrying that you have ruined your life, and your ex-Libran is having all the fun. As you might have gathered by now, this is unlikely. Your ex might be as upset as you.

Your emotional healing therefore needs to incorporate the Water element.

As you are capable of weeping for the world, the next time you are in floods of tears capture one small teardrop and place it into a small glass. Have one handy just for this purpose. Decorate it if you feel like it. Small flowers, stars, or twinkly things.

Now fill your glass to the top with tap water and place it on a table.

Then recite the following:

'This loving relationship with you ... (Libran's name) has ended.
I reach out across time and space to you.

My tears will wash away the hurt I feel.
I release you from my heart, mind and soul.
We part in peace.'

And then slowly drink the water. Imagine your hurt dissolving away, freeing you from all anxieties and releasing you from sadness. Then spend the next few weeks being nice to yourself. If you need to talk, find someone you trust and confide in them. Keep tissues handy.

Your Libra Friend

I have a number of very nice Libra friends. They are polite, well turned out and concerned about current affairs. Most of my Libra friends are also very well read and up to date with what's happening in the world.

One lovely Libra lady I used to work with, after the birth of my baby, wanted to get me a present, and spent numerous hours thinking about something suitable. She was working on the assumption that to buy a present for someone who couldn't have chocolates, had hay fever and who doesn't drink alcohol was difficult...but it didn't stop her from being very creative.

A few days after the birth when I'd come home, a package arrived. It was a small box and inside was a blue helium balloon with 'Congratulations! It's a boy!' written on it. How thoughtful! It was low-sugar, pollen-free, alcohol-free and floated around my living room for a number of days.

Sweet!

If you are friends with a Libra, make sure your relationship is give and take. Don't expect them to provide all the entertainment and equally don't smother them with your problems or with things you hate. Don't also spend too much time together as your friendship will soon wane. A happy Libra is, after all, quite an independent-minded individual and won't want smothering, so pay attention if you're a Water sign.

Your Libra Mum/Mom

A number of the Libra ladies I know are mums (moms) and like to be fair with their children.

Celia tells us about parenting her children:

'Being fair to my children means equal time, attention and handouts – I never had siblings so always try to keep the peace and make sure I am open and honest with them. I would hate them to fall out or have a chip on their shoulder for something I have done or not done as I hear a lot about that from patients.'

Lola has two daughters and likes to be fair with them:

'With my two daughters I have always tried to give them the same things even though they are different people with different needs.'

Malina lives in Europe; English isn't her first language. She tells us about her mother:

'Mother is Libra and myself Aquarius. In early years I remember matters run quite smooth. She gave lot of freedom but she once said we (3 of us) wasn't much of troubles when young. Father was due to jobs much travelling so she was the one with the pants in home. I also remember she learned us to share fair. Everything was divided in 3 equal pieces, like candies or if one got something, like new clothes, we all got. And if not, like having a bicycle, that was explained with whys.'

Her mother was concerned with fairness, even going as far as dividing things into three equal pieces. She also explained why she'd done certain things, which is a skill all Libras have. They will always tell you 'why' they did something.

Not every person has a joyful story about his or her mother. Georgina is an Aquarius and works for a non-profit agency in

North Carolina:

> 'Growing up, I idolized her. She was a good mother. Permissive and protective, standing up for my brother and I even when we were wrong. Pinnacle points in my relationship with her are memories of times when she pulled me up from being on the verge of making a big mistake. She was able to turn the tides by talking to me and helping me to see the light when I needed it most.'

Unfortunately her mother fell apart when her father died and their relationship radically altered and now they don't speak to each other. As a Libra identifies themselves *through* their relationship with their partner, for their partner to die becomes the biggest tragedy. As Georgina is an Aquarius, she doesn't define herself through her relationship(s), so she wouldn't have felt the same sense of loss as her mother.

Chan is another Aquarius lady who lives in Beijing in China. Both her parents are Librans:

> 'We are getting on very well. The main characters I find relating to Libra through my parents: very balanced, graceful (don't go to extremes), artistic oriented and concerning justice. We share lots of talking for sure. However, as a Scorpio Moon, I might be more emotional or even over-tempered than "Weighing Libra", especially because they are not Water Moons. Other than that, our Suns are very compatible and supporting to one another.'

In one sense they get on well, but because Chan has a Scorpio Moon (a very intense Moon to have, see Chapter Four) she doesn't feel the same way as them.

Your Libra Dad

My grandfather was a Libra but unfortunately he died before I was born. I do know more about him than most people because he wrote a lot of letters to my father that my mother kept and wrote about in her book *Branching Out: Fruits of the Tree*.[16] My dad was posted in India during the Second World War.

Grandpa's letters were always very polite and caring. My dad was a Sagittarius with Moon in Libra and my grandfather was Libra with Moon in Sagittarius (two of my siblings have Moon in Sagittarius; it's a bit of a family thing!).

Here's my grandfather writing to my dad in November 1943. After talking about the promotion my dad had turned down, and a reminder that my grandmother had sent 'a month's supply of Tobacco through Messrs. Fribourg and Treyer' and various other bits of family information, he ends his letter:

> There is very little news to tell you of any import. I did write and acknowledge your lovely birthday letter to me and you should have received it by now. It is impossible to say how I appreciate it but I assure you I shall always treasure it. I too am looking forward to the day when I can take walks with you in some part of our beautiful England calling in on some nice country pub and having a nice pint or two of bitter. Those days are worth waiting for. We are both looking forward eagerly to the day when we can welcome you home again.
>
> There is a new road running from Sadiya in Northern India over the roof of the world to Chungking where it joins the Burma Road. What a place for a walk, when you get a holiday. I only wish I could come with you. What a place to spend your leave and what an experience.
>
> Much love, my darling, from us all.
> Daddy

Scott is a Capricorn with Moon in Libra. He tells us about his Libra father:

'My dad is Libra Sun. As a boy, I saw him as indestructible and rugged...but kinda lacking empathy and sensitivity. But he was a masculine dad and took me hunting and taught me a little about fixing cars. I saw how he had plenty of friends and was very outgoing. Overall our relationship was good.

But as an adolescent and then later, when I would try to work with him on projects, he was always so concerned with perfection. It was the cause of much frustration on my part. Still, I saw and valued his strengths. I began to understand his difficult life and decisions involving his relationship with "another woman" and my mother.

Now we look at each other and see strengths and weaknesses. We are different in our values but the same in our difficulty with decisions. He says, "Yes, son...decisions, decisions, decisions. It's the hard part of life."

I smile and think...Libra Sun.'

To get the best from your Libra dad, make sure you are polite, interested in them and what they're doing; lots of pleases and thank-yous go down well. Depending on what sign you are, you'll either get on really well, or you will struggle. The Water and Earth signs are more likely to find it difficult.

Your Libra Sibling

If you have a brother or sister who is Libra, or a half-sibling or even a step-sibling, you must pay attention to what sign and element you are.

If you're a fellow Air sign you'll get on well. There may be tons of arguments and you might not totally agree on everything, but you'll defend your Air sign sibling to the death unless you've got some seriously complicated Ascendants or Moons.

If you're a Fire sign it'll be either love...or hate. Nothing in-between. You also might find it slightly more difficult if you're an Aries as you're opposite signs, but with work you can get on.

If you're an Earth sign, you might find your Libra sibling very hard to understand (unless you're up on Astrology). Your priorities will be completely at odds. You want practical advancement and things like food, comfort and money to be assured. Your Libra sibling doesn't have that same priority, so you might find you ignore each other as a Libra might not find you 'interesting' enough.

If you're a Water sign, things can be more tricky.

Here's a young Pisces lady discussing her sister.

'My Libra sister is constantly talking and bragging about herself. She never cares about anything that has to do with me or my life. She makes me listen to her read her own birth chart for hours every day. She badgers me every second of the day to do things for her and keep her company. She never acknowledges when I do anything nice or any of my good qualities. SHE IS MEAN. And sometimes I think she is crazy. I am a Pisces.'

What I liked most about her online question (she was asking how to get on better with her sister) were the replies:

'That's sooo funny because I'm a Pisces, my older sister is a Libra, and I have always had the same problem. What I would do is take a break from her for a while or every so often. She may get upset due to the lack of attention and may even try to bully you here and there, but stay strong and tell her you need some breathing space. She'll be okay, so don't worry about her.'

This young lady is a Cancer:

'Libras are self-absorbed – period. Just harden up to her, treat her like she's not even your sister for a while. Don't answer her phone calls, don't sit next to her on the couch, leave the room whenever she enters, never say hi or look her in the eye, only talk to her when you *have to, and definitely no hugging. That's what I do to deal with problematic Libras. But it may be easier for me to shy away from someone since I'm a crab; I've been doing it to mean people for as long as I can remember: my father, brother, cousins, classmates. Believe me, after a while it starts to drive them mad, and then they'll try to get on your good side again.'*

If you read between the lines, the Pisces was complaining her sister was crazy and the Cancer lady's solution was 'no hugging'. That made me laugh as both of them were suggesting solutions **based on their own signs**.

For a Pisces to feel better about something, they need lots of time on their own, away from the 'thing' that's upsetting them. A Cancer needs to be hugged when things get bad, as tactile contact makes them feel SO much better. So the solution for Water signs is: an Air sign will never *feel* the way you do, so just trust your own feelings but don't expect your Libra sibling to feel as emotional as you – about anything – and make sure you don't spend too much time together.

Yes, a Libra likes company, which is what was happening with the Pisces lady's sister, but in being together all the time she was also experiencing her sister's less positive side.

If you like someone and you get on well, be with them as long as things are good. As the saying goes, you can choose your friends but you can't choose your family. You have to live in close proximity to your siblings, so make sure you do spend time on your own and don't try and 'correct' all the things you think are wrong or bad about them. It won't get you anywhere.

* * *

I hope you have enjoyed learning a little about the Sun sign Libra.

I am writing this while Saturn is in the sign of Libra, helping us learn about being fair in a responsible way, in my home/office in Bath, the hot-spring city in south west England. I am a Pisces. I am happy with my job, with my lovely son, my wonderful husband and my extensive family. I am especially grateful for all the kind people who gave me their thoughts and opinions for this book and helped in a myriad of other ways.

I know that all life is made from good and bad and I decided not so long ago to focus on the good.

There is a candle burning beside me and I am imagining that the flame is burning to help you focus on the good too.

If we all understood each other a little better, maybe we'd get on better.

I wish you all the peace in the world...and happiness too.

In Peace

Mary

www.maryenglish.com

Further Information

The Astrological Association
www.astrologicalassociation.com
The Bach Centre, The Dr Edward Bach Centre, Mount Vernon,
Bakers Lane, Brightwell-cum-Sotwell, Oxon, OX10 0PZ, UK
www.bachcentre.com
Ethical Dating Site www.natural-friends.com
Spiritual Community in North Scotland www.findhorn.org

Chart information and birth data from astro-databank at
www.astro.com and www.astrotheme.com

Example Charts

Marc Edmund Jones, 1st October 1888, St Louis MO, USA,
8.37am, Scorpio Asc, Sun in 11th, Moon Leo

Caroline W Casey, 14th October 1952, Washington DC, USA,
1.38pm, Capricorn Asc, Sun in 9th, Moon Virgo

Ascendant

Martina Navratilova, 18th October 1956, Prague, Czech Republic,
4.40pm, Aries Asc, Sun in 7th, Moon Aries

Sigourney Weaver, 8th October 1949, Manhattan NY, USA,
6.15pm, Taurus Asc, Sun in 6th, Moon Taurus

Cliff Richard, 14th October 1940, Lucknow, India, 9pm, Gemini
Asc, Sun in 5th, Moon Aries

Jim Henson, 24th September 1946, Greenville MS, USA, 12.10am,
Cancer Asc, Sun in 3rd, Moon Capricorn

Britt Ekland, 6th October 1942, Stockholm, Sweden, 12.20am, Leo Asc, Sun in 2nd, Moon in Leo

Julie Andrews, 1st October 1935, Walton-on-Thames, UK, 6am, Virgo Asc, Sun in 1st, Moon Scorpio

Mahatma (Mohandas) Gandhi, 2nd October 1869, Porbanda, India, 7.11am, Libra Asc, Sun in 12th, Moon Leo

Margaret Thatcher, 13th October 1925, Grantham, England, 9am, Scorpio Asc, Sun in 12th, Moon Leo

Marc Bolan, 30th September 1947, Hackney, England, 12.30pm, Sagittarius Asc, Sun 11th, Moon Aries

Jesse Jackson, 8th October 1941, Greenville SC, USA, 2.15pm, Capricorn Asc, Sun in 9th, Moon Taurus

F Scott Fitzgerald, 24th September 1896, St Paul, MN, USA, 3.30pm, Aquarius Asc, Sun in 8th, Moon Taurus

Deepak Chopra, 22nd October 1946, New Delhi, India, 3.45pm, Pisces Asc, Sun in 8th, Moon Virgo

Moon Sign

Gore Vidal, 3rd October 1925, West Point NY, USA, 10am Scorpio Asc, Sun in 11th, Moon Aries

Dawn French, 11th October 1957, Holyhead, no birth time, Moon Taurus

Brigitte Bardot, 28th September 1934, Paris, France, 1.15pm, Sagittarius Asc, Sun in 10th, Moon Gemini

Graham Greene, 2nd October 1904, Berkhamsted, England, 10.20am, Scorpio Asc, Sun in 11th, Moon Cancer

Samuel Taylor Coleridge, 21st October 1772, Ottery St Mary, England, 10.45am, Sagittarius Asc, Sun in 11th, Moon Leo

Kate Winslet, 5th October 1975, Reading, England, 7.30am (unconfirmed time), possibly Libra Asc, Sun in 1st, definitely Moon in Libra

Louise Hay, 8th October 1926, Los Angeles, CA, USA, no birth time, Sun Libra, Moon Scorpio

Friedrich Nietzsche, 15th October 1844, Rocken, Germany, 10am, Scorpio Asc , Sun in 11th, Moon in Sagittarius

Michael Douglas, 25th September 1944, 10.30am, New Brunswick NJ, USA, Scorpio Asc, Sun in 11th, Moon in Capricorn

Florence Scovel Shinn, 24th September 1871, Camden, NJ, USA, no birth time, Sun Libra, Moon Aquarius

Marie Stopes, 15th October 1880, Edinburgh, Scotland, 4.10am, Virgo Asc, Sun in 1st, Moon Pisces

Houses

Stuart Wilde, 24th September 1946, Farnham, England, 6am (time given to me personally at a book signing in London) Virgo Asc, Sun in 1st, Moon Virgo

Oscar Wilde, 16th October 1854, Dublin, Ireland, 3am, Virgo Asc, Sun in 2nd, Moon Virgo

Anne Robinson, 26th September 1944, Liverpool, England,

11.45pm, Cancer Asc, Sun in 3rd, Moon Capricorn

Bruce Springsteen, 23rd September 1949, Freehold NJ, USA, 10.50pm, Gemini Asc, Sun in 4th, Moon Libra

Edith Stein, 12th October 1891, Breslau, Poland, 7.30pm, Gemini Asc, Sun in 5th, Moon Aquarius,

John Lennon, 9th October 1940, Liverpool, England, 6.30pm, Aries Asc, Sun in 6th, Moon in Aquarius

Stephen Arroyo, 6th October 1946, Kansas City MO, USA, 5.35pm, Aries Asc, Sun in 7th, Moon Aquarius

Jerry Lee Lewis, 29th September 1935, Ferriday LA, USA, 3pm, Aquarius Asc, Sun in 8th, Moon in Libra

Bob Geldof, 5th October 1951, Dublin, Ireland, 2.20pm, Sagittarius Asc, Sun in 10th, Moon Sagittarius

Thomas Moore, 18th October 1940, Detroit MI, USA, 9.23am, Scorpio Asc, Sun in 11th, Moon in Capricorn

Other Quotes and Other Famous Librans
Tracy Marks, 26th September 1950, Miami Beach, Florida, USA, 12.36pm, Sagittarius Ascendant, Sun in 10th, Moon Aries

R D Laing, 7th October 1927, Glasgow, Scotland, 5.15pm, Pisces Asc, Sun in 7th, Moon Aquarius

Suzanne Valadon, 23rd September 1865, Bessiness, France, 6am, Libra Asc, Sun in 12th, Moon Scorpio

Lillie Langtry, 13th October 1853, Isle of Jersey, no accurate birth time, Sun Libra, Moon Pisces

T.S. Eliot, 26th September, 1888, St.Louis MO, USA, 7.45am, Libra Asc, Sun in 12th, Moon Gemini

Edith Randall, 10th October 1897, Minneapolis, MN, USA, 6am, Libra Asc, Sun in 1st, Moon Aries

T.P. Ecob 'Orion', 9th October 1858, Melton Mowbray, England, 12.50pm, Sagittarius Asc, Sun in 10th, Moon Scorpio

Ann Noreen Widdecombe, 4th October 1947, Bath, UK, 10am, Libra Asc, Sun in 11th, Moon Taurus

References

1. Linda Goodman, *Sun Signs*, Pan Books, London, 1972
2. Christopher McIntosh, *The Astrologers and Their Creed: An Historical Outline*, Arrow Books, London, 1971
3. Rae Orion, *Astrology for Dummies*, IDG Books, Foster City CA, USA, 1999
4. YouGov survey http://labs.yougov.co.uk/news/2010/10/14/stars-their-eyes/
5. Diane Wolkstein and Samuel Noah Kramer, *Inanna, Queen of Heaven and Earth: Her Stories and Hymns from Sumer*, Harper Perennial, New York, 1983
6. Nick Campion, *The Dawn of Astrology*, 2 volumes, Continuum, London, 2009
7. David A. Aguilar, *11 Planets: A New View of the Solar System*, National Geographic Society, Washington DC, USA, 2008
8. Paul Sutherland, *Astronomy: A Beginner's Guide to the Sky at Night*, Igloo Books, Sywell, Northampton, 2007
9. Tracy Marks, *Planetary Aspects: From Conflict to Cooperation: Making Your Stressful Aspects Work for You*, CRCS Publications, USA and Canada, 1987
10. Liz Greene and Howard Sasportas, *The Inner Planets: Building Blocks of Personal Reality*, Seminars in Psychological Astrology Volume 4, Samuel Weiser, York Beach ME, USA, 1993
11. Caroline W. Casey, *Making the Gods Work for You: The Astrological Language of the Psyche*, Three Rivers Press, New York, 1998
12. Donna Taylor, *How to Use the Healing Power of Your Planets: Induce Better Health and Well-Being*, Quantum, Slough, Berkshire, 2003
13. Donna Cunningham, *How to Read Your Astrological Chart: Aspects of the Cosmic Puzzle*, Red Wheel/Weiser, York Beach

ME, USA, 1999

14. Thomas Moore, *Care of the Soul: How to Add Depth and Meaning to Your Everyday Life*, illustrated edition, HarperCollins, New York, USA, 1998

15. http://www.killerinthesun.com/index.php?option=com_content&task=view&id=61&Itemid=36

16. Jean English, *Branching Out: Fruits of the Tree*, self-published, 2002 www.jeanenglish.co.uk

Dodona Books offers a broad spectrum of divination systems to suit all, including Astrology, Tarot, Runes, Ogham, Palmistry, Dream Interpretation, Scrying, Dowsing, I Ching, Numerology, Angels and Faeries, Tasseomancy and Introspection.